The Power of

HOPE &

JOY

Jennifer O'Brien

Freedom Publishing
49 Kingmere, South Terrace
Littlehampton, BN17 5LD, United Kingdom

ISBN: 978-1-908154-70-5

British Library Cataloguing in Publication Data. A catalogue record for this book is available from the British Library

Unless otherwise stated all scripture quotations are taken from the New American Standard Bible®, Copyright © 1960, 1971, 1977, 1995, 2020 by The Lockman Foundation. All rights reserved.

Scripture quotations marked ESV are taken from The ESV® Bible (The Holy Bible, English Standard Version®). ESV® Text Edition: 2016. Copyright © 2001 by Crossway, a publishing ministry of Good News Publishers. The ESV® text has been reproduced in cooperation with and by permission of Good News Publishers. Unauthorized reproduction of this publication is prohibited. All rights reserved.

Scripture quotations marked NIV are taken from Holy Bible, New International Version® Anglicized, NIV® Copyright © 1979, 1984, 2011 by Biblica, Inc.® Used by permission. All rights reserved worldwide.

Scripture quotations marked TPT are from The Passion Translation®. Copyright © 2017, 2018, 2020 by Passion & Fire Ministries, Inc. Used by permission. All rights reserved. ThePassionTranslation.com.

Scripture quotations marked MSG are taken from THE MESSAGE, copyright © 1993, 2002, 2018 by Eugene H. Peterson. Used by permission of NavPress. All rights reserved. Represented by Tyndale House Publishers, Inc.

Formatted by Freedom Publishing
Cover by David Powell, Publish My Book UK
Printed in the United Kingdom

DEDICATION

To my beloved parents

Mum, you are the most inspiring woman I know, full of love,
sacrifice, and generosity.

To my late Dad, you brought a dignity and tenderness to my
situation I will always treasure.

All those years ago, we did not know how the journey would go
and wondered. Now here is its story, better than we could have
imagined. Thank you for all your help to get me here - I could not
have done it without you.

To my greatest love, Jesus. You navigated the way for me. I have
no adequate words of gratitude, but you know you have my heart.

Jennifer O'Brien

CONTENTS

Endorsements

As a minister of healing for nearly 25 years, you don't get to meet many people that can hold on to hope and joy despite the circumstances of life like Jennifer does. Having known Jennifer now for over ten years, she is an exemplary model of what it means to stand against all odds. I have met Jennifer on several occasions and having watched from a distance over the years she has been a rich source of encouragement to me. There's a saying that I like to use, 'If God is outside of time, then should we not be giving thanks for our miracle as if it's already happened?'

We truly need a hope and joy revolution. I love it when you read a book and know that the author walks the talk. Many people fail in joy, contentment, and enjoying the present because their contentment is purely in their miracle. Our contentment should be in Jesus.

I would highly recommend without hesitation that if you need an infusion of hope, joy. and contentment in the present, then you need to indulge yourself in this incredible read!

Chris Gore
Author: Apprehended Identity and
Walking in Supernatural Healing Power.

Jennifer O' Brien is one of this world's rare treasures. Having worked with her now over an extended period, and knowing her for many years, I have found her to be a true example of Biblical normality. Perhaps this is the highest accolade one can ever give to another human being! She is compassionate and merciful, having walked a road of needing to find that from Jesus. She is bold and tenacious. She sees in the Spirit realm with an accuracy and vividness that is quite unparalleled.

Time with Jennifer is time well spent. If you want to understand how to live life well, in the midst of its not-inconsequential trials, this book will take you deep on a journey to the feet of Jesus, to a version of Him that many of us sadly never discover in this lifetime.

We wholeheartedly and unreservedly endorse Jennifer and all she is!

Emma Stark
Founder/Leader, Global Prophetic Alliance
Core Leader, British Isles Council of Prophets

God truly has inspired Jennifer to write this book, 'The Power of Hope & Joy'. It is a wonderful journey of finding hope and joy through every circumstance she found herself in. Such faith and trust in the Lord's love.

We have known Jennifer for over 15 years. She is an incredible prophet of the Lord. A woman of God with impeccable character and humility. Words cannot describe our love and respect for her. You will be totally blessed as you journey with her in reading her book.

Ian & Jane McCormack
(aka Jellyfishman)

Honest, heartfelt, and deeply courageous, 'The Power of Hope & Joy' is a divinely inspired invitation to a life of abundance (hope-filled and joyful) made possible through union with Jesus Christ. Its message is that hope and joy, in a limitless supply, are available to anyone who wants it.

The message for me, was that we can be, we should be, God's carriers of hope and joy to a world steeped in hopelessness.

Jennifer's book is a timely reminder for all who call themselves followers of Christ that life is about going, representing Him wherever and in whatever state that we find ourselves.

Notwithstanding daily trials, Jennifer has discovered the joy in being used by God, being 'powerfully effective for God on the earth,' and her clear response to His timeless question 'Whom shall I send?' jumps off the book's pages. 'Here am I. Send me!' And in her response is another question to you and I, ...'Will you go also?'

Chizor Akisanya
Author: Complete in Him

The Lord often uses people and their stories in Him as His most prized messengers to a broken and disillusioned world and church. We see this most powerfully in the life, death and resurrection of our Lord Jesus Messiah. Jennifer, a prized friend of mine this past fifteen years, is another such messenger carrying a vital message for the church in this hour: that of overcoming, that of learning to thrive, that of falling deeper in love with God, against all odds.

Jennifer's story is at once piercing, heart-wrenching, immovably honest and beautifully vulnerable. It is ultimately a story of seemingly impregnable hope, joy and peace which defies circumstance and celebrates the daily grace of God who accompanies us through thick and thin and never leaves us.

The last days ecclesia is in a time of bridal preparation. I commend her story to you as a wonderful accompaniment to one such beautifying fire. Jennifer is one who walks with God and is a testimony to the truth that if we have Jesus, we have all we need.

Dominic Muir
Author: God hunger: Meditations from a life of longing
Author: Firebrand: Devotions from a Life of Burning

A powerful authentic and thought-provoking book on the joy and the deep character that there is to be found in walking with Jesus through suffering.

Here is a book that answers the existential question Why do we suffer? Written honestly, unflinchingly and extremely well, this is not a misery memoir, but a book full of humour and life. Jennifer is a masterful story teller and her character and indeed her joy shine through her unique voice.

Emily Barroso
Author: After the Rains

To know Jennifer is to love her. The Power of HOPE & JOY is beautifully written and truly transparent, charting her highs and lows with everything in between. It is an impacting read!

Jennifer's perspective on hope is one forged in the fire of trial and pursuit of understanding. Her insight on joy is fresh and exciting to read. "… the worst moments of my past were subsumed by joy. I realised then that joy, fierce and consuming as it is, is undefeated even by suffering."

Luellen Mayhew
Leader, Kingsgate London

INTRODUCTION

I did not intend my life's journey becoming a book. At least not way back. And even when the idea was mooted, I thought of all the books in the world and gifted authors who had written them and doubted I had anything to add.

But in spite of myself, I knew I had something to say, and increasingly felt compelled to say it. When it came to the how, writing seemed the most obvious first step. Which has led to this point and a completed book in your hands.

At its simplest, my message is that there is a measure of hope and joy available which enables every person, not only to get through life's difficulties, but to live in vibrant fullness. More and more I want to shout it, because I see little evidence we, humans, know this key truth. And I feel the urgent need for its telling.

Mental health struggles are at record levels, the horrors of war are distressingly on view around the world, and a disturbed chaos sounds from human hearts asking who they are and what they are living for. A troubling weight of heaviness bears down on humanity.

But as I have discovered, that does not have to be the case. The truth is that everything we need for life in its most expansive and purest sense is found in God, in Jesus. As He is limitless, He has unlimited supplies of everything we need for meaningful living.

Why do I single out hope and joy? Not because they are the only God qualities that are important for us to know but because, in my experience, they are our most powerful defence in the battle against despair and meaninglessness.

So, I uncoil the scroll of my story, describing the life events which forced me on a search for hope when I had none. I tell of a young woman's (my) diagnosis of serious disease driving like a tank through my dreams, my despair at the prospect of a life of sickness, of my wrestling with God about getting well, and my outrage at the cards life had dealt me. When I eventually hit heartache's floor, I describe my escape from bleakness and despair.

The book is not intended to be auto-biographical in the traditional sense. Of necessity I describe events as they occurred to frame the inward journey. I am also honest in talking about the painful things as well as my weakness along the way. Still, a central message is that hope, joy, and friendship with God are always on offer. They change everything.

In fact, I learned how astonishingly powerful they are and that there is no fire or trial that can destroy them because they live in the unchanging heart of God. If we connect with that, we can know them. Fortunately, that is always open.

Often, I want to weep when I see how little hope and joy people really know, both those who profess belief in God and those who do not. I am no expert and feel the sting of life when it comes as much as anyone else. But I have tasted enough of God's goodness to know if we reach deep in Him for hope, joy, and anything else we need, we will find them. Clothed thus in His nature we can be formidable, able to profoundly impact the world.

Now some years on at the other side of the journey, I can truthfully say I am a changed woman. I have learned to live deep and continually in hope and joy seeing an impact on my life I could never have imagined.

They are a magnet for life.

But beyond my own journey something far greater has stirred. It is an urgent cry that has awakened and will not be put to sleep. It clamours 'Open the gates of hope and joy to rescue the world from despair.'

I hope as you read further that will be your cry too.

1

RUDE AWAKENING

Be patient and tough; someday this pain will be useful to you.
Ovid

'I've got good news for you! We've looked again at the scan and there's no growth on your spine. You can go home.' The Doctor offered a broad smile at his announcement, inviting me to share the moment of jubilation.

But I did not. Share the moment that is. Instead, I became aware of a sick feeling in my stomach, a creeping panic.

I heard myself protesting, 'But yesterday I was told the MRI scan shows a growth on my spine. What about the tests you were going to do?' The tension in my voice was audible, a mix of rising fear and challenge, as if pleading, 'You must have made a mistake – there has to be a growth.'

He answered, 'Well, we have had a closer look and don't believe the shadow is a growth. Easy to make that mistake. These scans can be difficult to read. We wouldn't want to put you through the tests if it wasn't absolutely necessary and it's not.'

Another smile from the doctor but this time more forced, quizzical, possibly wondering at my response. I was not showing any signs of being relieved by his news, deflating for him no doubt as this must have been a good news moment in his day. But my next question struck at the heart of the issue, exposing my fear.

'Does this mean I have MS?' My strained question came almost as a whisper.

His reply was brusque. Was he irritated by our exchange or I oversensitive, a sense of impending disaster distorting my perception?

'I can't say. I'm a surgeon. You will need to see a neurologist which your GP will arrange'.

And that was how it began.

You do not know me yet but, if you are wondering what kind of strange person I was to seemingly 'want' to have a growth on my spine, I should paint something of the bigger picture to explain.

At the time, I was in my final year of law studies in York, England but, after months of ignoring warning signs, had been forced to admit something was not quite right with my health. Although I was not overly concerned, I had developed a slight limp in my right leg, my balance was somewhat 'off', and I often felt electric currents running up and down my body. At the urging of friends, I agreed to see a doctor.

That led to a visit to my GP who, encouragingly, conveyed no alarm about my presenting symptoms. However, on the basis that the electric currents were bothering me as she put it, she sent me for tests to check for nerve damage. What I particularly remember about those was the immensely cheerful clinician who performed them, running his thumb up and down the back of my feet as I sat on a bed. This caused my right foot to shake almost uncontrollably unlike the left. He seemed surprised.

'Are you feeling nervous or anxious?', he asked. An odd question I thought given my obvious ease chatting with him.

'No, I'm not,' I answered, half-laughing. And without further explanation he completed the tests telling me not to worry - my doctor would get the results.

But it was when I went back to the GP that I heard the marked change in tone. Her previous lightness had given way to seriousness, signalling I guessed the imminence of unwelcome news. Until then that possibility really hadn't crossed my mind.

'The results of the tests aren't quite what I hoped,' she began hesitantly. I could feel my face change, registering both surprise and confusion as she continued, 'which means we need to do more investigation to find out what is going on.'

Now I was unnerved by her response. 'That doesn't sound great.' I responded. 'Can you be straight and tell me what you suspect?' I asked.

It was then in rather sombre tones she told me there were three possible scenarios. The first, that there was a cancerous tumour on my spine, the second, that there was a non-cancerous tumour on my spine and the third, that I had a major neurological condition called multiple sclerosis (MS). Although none were desirable, in fact all were in the 'seriously bad news category', by my somewhat shocked reckoning the best option was the second. If that proved to be the case, she explained, the cure would be back surgery to remove the growth thus relieving pressure on nerves. That was likely to be causing the other symptoms which meant I should recover normal health if the surgery went well. A not unhopeful forecast I thought.

After that conversation, it was quickly on to investigation with an MRI scan and a return visit to the GP apparently to promising results. The scan suggested option two which meant the 'surgery plus full recovery route' seemed to be on offer.

When the GP first delivered the news, my huge relief must have been obvious as I remember her saying she hadn't ever seen a patient so pleased at the prospect of back surgery. Of course, I was not really pleased. It was a horrible, scary prospect with no guarantee the outcome would be the success I hoped. But when faced with three grim health scenarios, who would not be grateful that fate seemed to be meting out the least bad possibility. I even have a clear memory of going back to my student house that evening, dancing around my room in delight, particularly at the knowledge I did not have MS. Bizarrely, perhaps, cancer seemed less awful to me. Admittedly tough in its treatment and it might cut my life short but, in my mind, MS was likely to be a longer, lingering road of potentially horrible ill-health. A greater dread.

Her news was then followed by speedy admission to hospital as described only to be discharged by the surgeon a day later. By that point I had a sense of what was coming although still clung to the tiniest hope medics would find they had missed something simple. But regrettably to no avail. When I next saw the GP, it was to hear her devastating words that MS was the only disease they were now looking for.

As the GP outlined the subsequent medical steps, I will always be grateful for the wisdom and pragmatism she showed, recognising there was a lot at stake for me at that time with imminent law finals. She suggested I delay the necessary tests until after finals to minimise the chance of me flunking them due to upsetting news. There would be challenge enough for me in simply keeping my focus to study she said. If I could not and failed but turned out not to have MS, I would have derailed my future unnecessarily. But even if I did have MS, it would be better to do well in my finals in any event as who knew what would happen beyond diagnosis.

She was right and the plan worked. By some force of willpower, I managed to concentrate and study, while at the same time fight the lurking fear of something awful being about to happen. But those final months felt surreal. Once news got around the student community about my situation, I was met with a mix of reactions from reassurance, 'It'll probably be nothing.', to undisguised horror, 'Oh God, what a nightmare…', to awkward conversations where no-one mentioned it. The horror reaction was the worst; seeing other people scared of what you might have makes it even scarier. I did understand that everyone was being as kind as they knew how but they didn't know what would help and, honestly, neither did I.

Sadly, I had now detached from them and the extremely happy year it had been in York. The energy-infusing camaraderie of a bunch of students facing finals, that collective push to the finishing line, had left me behind. My focus now was getting to the end without being overwhelmed by the prospect of a life-changing diagnosis, while theirs was looking towards successful legal careers. Not the finale I had been expecting.

I heard someone once say that we do what we need to survive. True or not, unconsciously that is what I did. I seemed to create two spaces on the inside; I will call them warehouses. The upper warehouse was where all my legal learning was crammed in the run up to finals, along with the resources I drew on to keep myself functioning. The lower warehouse was where the shockwaves swirled around and the emotional Jennifer lived. It was full of fear and angst about my future, all held together by as firm a padlock as I could find to contain it and prevent me obsessing about grim health scenarios ahead. Surprisingly, these temporary internal structures seemed to work. I did not fall apart before finals. I managed to study. And when finals came, somehow, I was able to keep my head sensing I had done okay.

After that it was into hospital to conclusively establish if I had MS. The test was a spinal lumbar puncture which involves taking fluid from the spinal cord. Although it is not fun, I was reassured no one needed to be with me as I would only be in hospital for a night. Unfortunately, things did not go to plan. I reacted badly to it which meant the one-night stay in hospital turned into a week as my lumbar puncture headache raged without end.

But it was not the procedure or extended inpatient stay which left a nasty scar. It was something else. The patients in my ward were all very sick, but I particularly noticed the elderly woman in the bed opposite me. She was in the most advanced stages of MS which meant she was completely paralysed; unable to swallow or speak although she had not lost her sight. During the week, I felt nothing but compassion for her. It was achingly sad to witness, not only her plight, but that of her husband too. He visited every day and I could not help but see and hear something of the pain of those times. He forced an exaggerated cheerfulness into his voice as he tried to engage in a form of conversation with her. I winced. It was like a hand offered for a handshake to someone who does not have a hand to offer back. The false brightness sharply jarred with the palpable heaviness around her bed.

That week I often wondered what she was thinking in the numerous times our eyes met. Was she envying me my relative-good health at that point? Or was she feeling compassion I might face the same journey as she when she heard medical staff avoiding my questions about MS? Regardless, it was beyond inappropriate for me to have been put in a bed near her at that time, witnessing the worst consequences of MS when I was still daring to hope I would not have the disease. So, although reason told me this woman's MS outcome was not necessarily the norm, it was a hard picture to forget, imprinted on my mind as it was at such a vulnerable time.

After discharge, I had a two week wait for the neurologist appointment which would tell all. Finally, the day came. It was mild, the kind of overcast northern English summer day which refuses to give heat but has left the extremes of winter behind. It seemed ordinary but it was not.

Arriving early, I soon heard the words, 'Jennifer O'Brien?' My name rang out in the patient room as the nurse scanned waiting faces for a reaction. I got up catching her eyes and followed meekly. Everything felt like it was happening in slow motion. I wondered if she knew the enormity of the occasion. I felt the urge to shout out to the faces in the waiting room, 'Don't you know I'm about to find out if I have MS?' But I didn't.

Needless to say, I had been dreading this moment. Ever since my hope was snuffed out of removal of a spinal growth being the remedy for my ailments, I tried to brace myself for the diagnosis I did not want. Yet when the day of disclosure came, somewhere deep in my soul I could hear hope still gasping for air, whispering 'It might not be what you think'. But I hardly dared trust hope's whispers again for fear I would be let down.

'I'm sorry to confirm the indications are you have MS,' the neurologist began. The words I did not want to hear. Funny how a few sound waves can completely change one's reality. In just a few seconds, I had gone from being 'young healthy Jennifer' to 'Jennifer with a serious neurological disease'.

After those initial words, I kind of numbed out. I remember her parting comment however, 'It's not the terrible disease that many think; lots of people do very well with it.' But I did not believe her. To me, it was the worst possible news. After all, I knew where this diagnosis might lead.

Before you decide my response was melodramatic, I should put the MS label into context as it fell on my ears. I did not know anyone with MS, there was no history of it in my family, and thankfully we had all enjoyed good health as far back as I could remember. But my sense of the catastrophe that MS could loose on my life still wasn't without basis.

For starters, I was familiar with the devastating story of the cellist, Jacqueline du Pré. She was and remains one of the all-time greats, part of the golden couple of classical music married to Daniel Barenboim, and particularly famed for her performances of the Elgar cello concerto. Yet her career and life were tragically cut short by MS. At only 28 years, and with an astonishing talent, the effects of MS brought an end to concert giving as her hands began to lose function. She died in 1987 aged only 45 years.

Added to that backstory was my then recent experience of the older woman in hospital and shocking confrontation with what might be ahead for me.

Therefore, with these stories in mind and, admittedly, a limited lens on the world of MS, my fear was that it would grip and ruin my life as it had theirs. Now all its horrible possibilities were on offer to me; numbness in my body, paralysis, incontinence, being wheelchair bound, losing the ability to speak and swallow.

The horror of what might be.

2

ORIGINS

When anyone asks me about the Irish character, I say look at the trees. Maimed, stark and misshapen, but ferociously tenacious.

Edna O'Brien

I need to back up somewhat at this point to tell you who I am and what kind of life brought me here.

I am Irish, Dublin-born, but spent the earliest years of my childhood in Derry in the north of Ireland. As neither of my parents were from the north, that was unusual. Dad hailed from County Kilkenny and Mum from County Clare, but it was at university their paths crossed whilst studying dentistry. It was rather remarkable that in the late 1950s Mum studied dentistry. She says this was entirely due to her enlightened father. Once he realised she did not want to be a teacher or nurse, the main female occupations of the time, he urged her to do something else. Rare for a man of his time!

As a young father, Dad worked as a hospital registrar in Derry which was what brought us there as a family. It was during the time of 'The Troubles' as they were known, with all the awful division and violence between Catholics and Protestants. Young though I was, it rather amazes me that my memories of those times are still so keen; the sound of bombs exploding, security evacuations from school, and everyday lengthy car queues at British soldier checkpoints. But despite the environment, I was aware my parents were very happy there although their pragmatism eventually won the day. Thinking ahead, they decided the tense atmosphere of the north was not where they wanted to raise their children, so, when Dad was offered a consultant post as an oral surgeon in Cork, we moved.

Cork, in the Republic of Ireland, was where I spent most of my childhood. It is in the south of the south which means we get plenty, if not too much, rain from the Atlantic Ocean. As a result, we Irish, particularly those who live on the coast, are inordinately appreciative of even the briefest spell of dry, sunny weather.

I was one of three siblings; my sister, Marion, was two years older than me and my brother, Rory, two years younger. For my sister and I, the biggest adjustment from the move was our having to learn Irish (or Gaelic) at school; compulsory in the south but not the north. I was young enough to pick it up fairly quickly given my classmates had not had too much of a head start, but poor Marion had to figure out this new language at age ten when her classmates had begun it at five.

As siblings, I think we have always been quite close. My memory when very young, disputed by them of course, is that it was always Rory and Marion teaming up against me in our childhood tiffs! Marion has a quieter nature than I, but we were a good balance to each other. In contrast to me, her leaning at school was towards the sciences, which eventually led to her becoming a doctor.

Most of the time, we happily shared a bedroom. But an admittedly extremely petty frustration of mine was her refusal to chat with me at night. In my world, a little joint debrief of the day's events was a necessary cadence to its end but annoyingly not to her. Her refusal to talk when lights were off infuriated me, and held out even against my questions, exaggerated stories, or anything else I could think of to provoke conversation. Instead, her Mary Poppins-like steely resolve was always the same; that she was going to sleep and could I just be quiet! Funny how these childhood niggles maintain their record decades on. While visiting her home just a few years ago, I slept in her double bed with her (she was by then sadly widowed). As she turned out the lights, it felt like we had suddenly gone back in time to our teenage years. But no sooner had I drawn breath to speak in the dark, than I heard that familiar tone, 'Jen, I'm not talking to you. I'm going to sleep.' The same unbending determination. I thought she might have forgotten…

Rory was a different story. When very young, I had no interest in his boyish toys and games and, when he made it to his teens, I bemoaned the fact that he was not an older brother with potentially interesting older friends. But it was as young adults that things changed. He had studied economics at university, which took him to working in a bank in London. By chance, I also found myself in London at the beginning of my legal career by which time childish quibbles were far behind us. Feeling the acute blow of the MS diagnosis, I was grateful for his maturity and calm as he made light of my worst imaginings to turn my mood. No deep philosophical thought; just, 'Sure don't be worrying about that, it might never happen.' And so often just the words were balm enough.

Looking back, I had a good life. I enjoyed school, had great friends, and discovered by accident I appeared to be an above average violinist and pianist. From enrolment by Mum in early piano and violin lessons, I fell in love with classical music. To my parents' credit not having musical backgrounds themselves, they encouraged and facilitated my passion. They took me to endless lessons and rehearsals, funded trips away, and rode with me the rollercoaster of triumphs and disappointments in my classical music world. What they probably were not expecting, however, was my decision mid-secondary school to pursue a career as a violinist. For my security their instinct was to steer me in the direction of a more traditional career which meant they insisted I apply myself at school in case music did not work out. But subject to that proviso, they were fully behind me.

Actually, keeping a focus on studies was not a hardship for me. I enjoyed secondary school. The Irish curriculum was commendably wide which meant I got to dip my toes in many subjects. I was also a keen debater, though that diminished in later years as music took over. But I see now that many of the things I am passionate about today, language, poetry, being a voice, a communicator, had some of their seeds planted in that school season.

In those formative years, I also saw my faith in God grow and figure large in my life, even if very privately held. Typical for my generation in Ireland, I had grown up as a Church-going member of the Catholic Church as did all my friends. From a young age, I had been taught that God was a loving Father who sent His son, Jesus, to die in my place for the forgiveness of my sins. But what I knew about God was not just head information to me. Although I cannot entirely explain why, there was more to it for me. I recall having a certainty about God's existence and a sense of His being with me. While there might have been gaps in my understanding of exactly how Jesus' death and resurrection enabled me to connect with God, there was still something deeply laid in my heart about Him. I knew He was the truth I needed to follow, that He loved me, and that I could trust Him as the rock of my life.

In my teenage years, my curiosity about God only grew but now with a desire to experience Him. After all, if He actually was a Father, friend, and brother, He must be inherently relational. That being so, surely, I could expect to experience Him as seen in the lives of early church figures like Peter, Paul, and Stephen who had wonderful and frequent encounters with Him. In fact, the experience of all the early church with Him was up-close and personal; sick people routinely healed, angels rescuing people from prison, and believers hearing God's voice continually. I was provoked by their lives.

My dilemma was that I did not know people who encountered Him in such a direct way. But after some time telling God I was eager for more, I heard His answer or, at least, its beginnings. It came in the form of a book recommended by a teacher. Called 'Run Baby Run', it was penned by Nicky Cruz, a notorious Puerto-Rican born gang leader who had a dramatic and life-changing encounter with Jesus. This resulted in him coming out of the destructive life he lived into real relationship with Jesus, effecting life-long change of heart and character.

I remember the moment of impact of the book vividly. It occurred on a day I mistakenly took the wrong bus from school, forcing a two-mile walk home. I was so gripped by the book's opening chapter that, walking or not, I determined to keep reading. On a winding country lane with the sun streaming through the trees speckling light across the pages, I read about Nicky's encounter with Holy Spirit or the spirit of God[1]. As Nicky invited God into his life, he described the cleansing he felt from the stain of the terrible things he had been involved in, as well as the overwhelming love of Jesus filling him. It was as life-changing in description as any Bible story I had read, but more riveting, and the first time I had come across anyone living describe such an encounter. As I read, my heart was agog with interest and longing. I found myself wanting to offer my life to God in similar, whole-hearted terms, asking Jesus to be Lord of my life. Like Nicky, I grasped that real life was only to be had in receiving Jesus' forgiveness for my sins and then giving my life to Him. So, I yielded, knowing Holy Spirit came to live in me as I did. I knew that was my assurance I would live eternally with Him, as well as in fullness of life with Him now. Or put another way, it was my moment of becoming 'born again' as the Bible describes; my choice of a new life in and with God.

Unlike Paul on his way to Damascus, in the moment I did not see a great light or hear an audible voice. But I nevertheless felt an inward confidence something had happened, that God had heard me. That prayer, my earliest firm decision to live my life walking with God, also put a seal on my hunger to know Him in a way that was not just theoretical, even if the desire was not satisfied in my teenage years. If I am honest, my faith journey in Ireland was lonely. My friends did not seem to share my curiosity. Nevertheless, I determined to pursue what was in my heart certain God would not give me a desire for something He didn't want to impart. As King David himself scribed *'my soul will be satisfied as with fat and rich foods,'* (Psalm 63:5 ESV). Later I would discover how right I was.

Once I had made up my mind that music was my future, I was given the opportunity to spend a year studying violin in Vienna, Austria. The chance to be a student at age nineteen in a foreign country was appealing enough in itself, but to study music in the Mecca of the classical music world, where the greats of the past had lived and left their shadows, could not be refused. On top of that, I had loved German at school so jumped at the chance to live in the German speaking world for a season.

Not surprisingly, Vienna did not disappoint. It is a magical city and I was fortunate to live near its centre, beside the famous 'Karlskirche'. The thrill of passing this stunning, floodlit church on my way home each evening never left me, as compellingly beautiful in the hot, balmy summer evenings as when it was blanketed in thick winter snow. Vienna was full of adventure to me, made more intoxicating doubtless because it was my first year away from home. From studies with an eminent violinist and immersion in classical music to mixing with new people and improving my German, I loved it all. To this day, it feels like I left a little bit of Jennifer there. Something in me has always loved the

German speaking world and, even on the final evening, I felt the press of sadness as I wandered around the city in the early hours willing the year not to end.

But despite these mixed emotions, I had known its conclusion was coming and planned accordingly. After audition, I had happily been accepted into the Royal Northern College of Music in Manchester, UK for undergraduate studies with the violinist, Yossi Zivoni. Following Manchester, I planned to go back to Vienna or somewhere else equally far-flung for postgraduate studies.

I had my future planned, or so I thought.

Notes

[1] Holy Spirit is part of the three persons of God or Trinity, Father, Son and Holy Spirit, which make up the one God.

3

MISADVENTURE

Ever tried. Ever failed. No matter.
Try Again. Fail again. Fail better.
Samuel Beckett

Being at the Royal Northern was great, even if a different experience to Vienna. What was lost by moving in the aesthetic and musical history of a city, was more than made up for in a wonderful teacher and structured course. It offered a more rounded education than Vienna, a mix of academic content with performance which suited me well. It also led to my joining a very good string quartet. And to top it all, I made the most wonderful friends.

As a string quartet, we periodically gave recitals around the country. One such concert took place in the north of England on a particularly cold winter evening in my third year. Once my fellow musicians and I returned to Manchester by train, we made our way to the main road, in high spirits the concert had gone well. In giddy mood then Owen, our violist, and I decided to run down the icy road we were walking on. It was hardly a reckless act – just a bit of fun - but resulted in Owen skidding landing on top of me.

'Ouch', I heard myself yelling as a shot of pain went through my left hand under his weight. He quickly got up checking I was okay and, after a few minutes establishing I could still move my fingers, we concluded it was nothing a few days' rest wouldn't fix.

But how wrong I was.

Rather unbelievably, within a year this tiny incident put an end to my hopes of life as a violinist. Very quickly I developed continuous, low-level back pain which no amount of physio, osteopathy, or anything else seemed to fix notwithstanding my pleas to God for help. I tried different approaches for cure from sleeping on the floor instead of my appalling student bed to not playing at all during treatment before beginning to play again for repeated short periods. But as soon as I began to play for more than twenty minutes, the persistent backpain returned.

Against that background Yossi talked to me about the future at the end of the year. His concern was that things were only likely to get worse if I continued with an injury which would probably force me to stop playing eventually. So, painful and momentous though the decision was, I found myself agreeing that pursuit of a playing career no longer made sense without signs of likely improvement ahead. Although I could see the logic of the decision - cutting my losses then to begin carving out a different future - it was still shocking to me. I had no vision for life without music; it had been my joy and driver. Without it I could not comprehend what life would be like.

People often ask me how I coped with this setback. Looking back, I was quite frozen in my response to it. I did not cry much, collapse in a heap with friends, or even express great sadness about invested years seeming to come to nothing. I knew they thought it slightly strange. So did I, although I did not understand it. But with the passage of time, I do. Post injury I actually felt quite defeated, not only by the failed efforts at cure, but also the historic accumulation of aspirations dashed. When I went to Vienna, I already felt underdeveloped as a musician by comparison with students who had given music more time in their youth by attending special music schools or cutting back on mainstream school. Because of that, I had to work hard to catch up. But the interruption of this latest saga caused me to lose yet another year of development. I was even more demoralised.

That said, I was still hugely upset at the turn of events, bewildered that the musical life I had envisioned was at an end. But emotion had to be set aside in order to figure out what I should do next. That decision became switching to the Royal Northern's academic music degree to complete my studies with an extra year to fill in the learning gaps.

Once I finished my degree, the following two years saw me teaching violin in schools in the Manchester area. There are some who love teaching that age group - after all, there are those who taught me. But I quickly learned it did not suit me. So, in some desperation to find new direction, I looked at postgraduate options. I clearly recall the decisive day. Settled comfortably in Manchester's main library, I was scouring directories listing courses. Nothing sparked my interest until I got to law. To my amazement, I discovered that two years of postgraduate legal studies in England would set me on the road to becoming a lawyer because I already had a degree. But even more surprising was my reaction. Inside I felt a sort of jump, as if my heart did a happy somersault. Could this be the future for me?

You may well wonder why a move to law would pique my interest after a life immersed in music. In fact, it was not quite the leap you might think as law had always been next on my list of career choices had music not worked out. As fantastically creative as classical music is, it is full of structure and order in common with law. Legal work also requires a love of language and expression which were similarly passions of mine. I love words. Of course, once I chose music, I never expected law to feature in my life, but now that the dice of life had been thrown in a different direction for me, it appeared it might.

Still slightly nonplussed, I decided to push on doors to see what happened, asking God to open them if law was a fit for me. To my surprise, they opened quickly. From the 'phone call with Mum and Dad saying they would support me if I wanted to go back to university, to getting multiple late offers of university places for that academic year, there seemed to be a big yes around law written in the heavens for me. That was underscored by my getting a much-coveted training contract with a London firm shortly after. That is a kind of two-year apprenticeship with a law-firm; necessary for qualifying as a solicitor, but hugely difficult to come by at the time.

So here I was. Yes, the dream of a musical career had rather imploded, but a path into law had fairly effortlessly opened up.

Honestly, I was in awe of God's goodness in offering me a new field of study when the only one I knew had closed. It would be a whole new world. For the first time in a few years, in fact since my injury, I felt excited about the future.

4

LIMPING AND FALLING

You never know how strong you are until
being strong is your only choice.
Bob Marley

That then is how life took me to legal studies in York before an MS diagnosis. But brutal though it was I discovered life doesn't stop even for our crises. Diagnosed in July, by the end of the month I heard I had passed my exams. Relief at the news, however, quickly gave way to worry about next steps. The London job would begin in September, but I was still reeling from the shock of it all. I could not fathom how I would face the demands of a new city, new job, new life. I was overwhelmed.

Decisions had to be made quickly however. When considering my options, I decided I should not throw the training contract away without attempting it. If I tried to do the job and failed, at least I would know I had tried. If I did not, there was no other obvious path immediately available to me and I might forever regret my decision. So I moved to London. To help in the transition, my dear Aunt Freda and Uncle Gearóid kindly invited me to live with them for those initial months in London. Their generosity was an absolute lifesaver for which I am forever grateful. Without the safety net of their support, I might have bottled out. It is true to say I did not because of it.

In the week before beginning my job, Freda took me clothes shopping for an office wardrobe. Whether she planned it with that in mind or not I do not know, but it was a great diversion from anxiety, forcing me away from obsessing about the imagined challenges ahead. And as I mixed and matched tops and suits, occasionally I even forgot my woes as I enjoyed our outings. Then abruptly and randomly, I would recall the ominous news, feeling the jolt of a new shock. I have since learned that is a common reaction to traumatic events. One forgets at times as a means of coping and then remembers again, sometimes with a greater sense of shock than before coupled with guilt for the brief mental reprieve. Even the coping mechanism has its own poison.

When my first day came, Freda dropped me at the train station, very nervous about being able to manage the journey. It involved getting a train to London Bridge in rush hour and from there walking three hundred metres to the firm's offices on Clink Street. Day one would show whether it was even doable. But I was determined if nothing else, so, leaning on my walking stick as if my life depended on it and with slow steps, I embarked on the walk arriving at the office on time. When I did, I could have cried with relief at the mountain climbed, but instead managed to force the emotions down as the receptionist asked my name, before ushering me to the room with the other trainees. No time to indulge my triumph.

Within minutes we were joined by someone else. 'Hello ladies, I'm Nick – delighted to welcome you to the firm!' His voice was warm as he shook each of our hands smiling reassuringly explaining he was the partner responsible for trainees. There were three of us in this intake I learned, me, Katie and Emily, all officially beginning our training contracts that morning.

'Once you've had the grand tour of the office, we should go for some lunch,' he continued. 'I've booked us a table at a nearby restaurant on Tooley Street. Shouldn't take us a minute to walk there and you'll meet the second-year trainees who'll join us.'

With that, Nick cast a glance at my walking stick showing no surprise. No doubt he had been filled in on the story of the new trainee with MS. Before my training began, I arranged a meeting with the firm to tell them the news. I had decided to be open about my situation although in reality I did not have a choice. Using a walking stick was a giveaway as well as not being able to manage a walk of more than 300 metres once in a day, and that only at a huge push. In the two months since diagnosis my ability to manage distance had drastically reduced, along with deterioration to my balance hence reliance on a stick. I knew if I was not up front before I began, I would have to be when I did.

Turning slightly towards me, he asked in lowered tones if I would be ok walking, repeating it was very close. But I did not know. I was no more expert than he in understanding what I could and couldn't manage in this unfamiliar world of MS. I did know I could walk for a minute. But was the restaurant really just a minute away or more like five, casually expressed in the non-specific way I used to when precise distance did not matter?

Unsurprisingly, I was daunted by my first day; trying to make a good impression, completely new to the office world (who was this person in a suit?), horribly self-conscious about my stick, and convinced this experiment of trying to become a lawyer would fail. Certainly, I did not have the confidence to ask for a taxi.

Instead, I heard myself timidly acquiescing, 'I'm sure it'll be fine.'

Yes, it was, in that I made it to the restaurant but no, it was not, in that I could barely walk. Lunch, therefore, was quite agonising as I tried to physically recover from the walk while making conversation with new people. At the same time, I was panicking inside about how I would manage the walk back. Stressful to say the least.

Thus were the beginnings of my time as a trainee with Warner Cranston, later to become US firm Reed Smith. Those two years are still vividly etched in my mind. I call it my 'big daze phase' because I lived it in a daze of sorts.

Of course, for any rookie lawyer it is a challenging time. Trainees are full of book knowledge but no practical experience as they arrive fresh from law school. They are trying to impress experienced colleagues all the time, as well as compete for the prize of a qualified lawyer job at the end. An intense and pressured environment for anyone. But for me, struggling physically and in constant fear of how MS might develop, a time of immense pressure trying to function and perform in the job.

To its credit, Warner Cranston was both sympathetic and well-disposed towards me. In fact, individually and collectively the partners, lawyers, and support staff were all really good to me. If I am honest, I wondered if they might look for the first opportunity to let me go. But I never felt they were waiting for me to fail or get sick or that they treated me any different to the other trainees. As much as anyone else, I was included in challenging legal work and client meetings. In fact, every consideration was afforded me to make the job workable such as taking taxis to meetings for even tiny distances if necessary and, later, finding me a parking space near the office so I could drive to work. Equally, no consideration was afforded me to require less of me as a lawyer which was exactly what I wanted. Challenging though my circumstances were, I wanted to be trained the same as everyone else and, if I qualified, for it to be on equal terms.

Aside from the general goodwill towards me, there were also frequent fun moments with my peers which provided welcome relief from the internal stress I worked hard to hide. Innumerable kindnesses were shown to me by colleagues which register large in my mind to this day even if forgotten by them. I learned then that the smallest kindness shown someone, especially in fragile moments, can be profoundly life-giving, its uplifting affects felt long after the event. Some of those kindnesses literally kept me going in those early dark days.

Two gestures stand out. Once a month, all us lawyers would attend a lunchtime meeting to discuss caseloads and the law. At the time, my office was on the floor below the meeting room. My colleagues on the upper and lower floors all used the short stairs to go to the meeting while I used the lift. At the end of one meeting, I was among the first to leave and stood beside the lift waiting for its arrival. One by one, my colleagues silently trooped past me to take the stairs to their offices. It should not have been an awkward moment – everyone knew why I took the lift – but somehow on this day there was a slight self-consciousness about it as colleagues passed me, their vigorous MS-free steps loud on the wooden floor. Sensing someone behind me, I turned around. To my surprise, Dave, a fellow lawyer, was standing there, also waiting for the lift.

'Why aren't you taking the stairs, Dave?' Is this a lazy streak I see coming out?' I teased.

In his warm northern Irish accent, he replied 'Ach, I've decided I need to conserve my energy, so much legal work to do today. Thought I would start by saving on walking.'

I was touched. We both knew that was not true. Dave was trying to relieve the aloneness of the moment for me by joining me. A tiny spontaneous gesture on his part, the decision to wait with me made in a nano second and, in the scheme of things, nothing really. But his sensitivity towards me was deeply touching. It felt like warm oil had been poured into my heart.

The other I call my hyacinth moment. It happened when I moved to the employment law department to work for a senior lawyer I was somewhat intimidated by, without reason I later discovered. Nervous, I arrived at her office hesitating at the door. She called out to me to come in and, as I did, I saw a hyacinth plant close to blooming on my desk.

'Welcome to the department,' she greeted. 'The hyacinth is for you, a gift to mark your arrival.'

She smiled warmly. I was taken aback. The gift was as unexpected as her amiability and, together, they seemed to collapse my fear somewhat. Much more unexpected though was the effect of the hyacinth on me that week. Day by day as it bloomed and the potency of its rich fragrance increased, it seemed to speak a wordless message of hope to me for my life despite the apparent ruins of MS around me. It reminded me of the prophet Isaiah's words *'the desert…. will burst into bloom'*.

She could not have imagined its effect and neither could I. That week, it felt like I inhaled hope when I was in the office. And this time it did not disappoint as my stint in that department was where I first began to find my feet as a lawyer - pun aside - to do well and begin to enjoy law. Even to this day when I smell a hyacinth, I am immediately brought back to the moment Alison told me it was for me, and the eruption of hope its perfume released in my soul.

A mystery, for sure, in the enduring weight of the smallest things.

But the reality of this time was that I was living in two very different states. One was the professional life Jennifer who was putting on a suit and forced smile to come to work as a trainee. The other was a deeply troubled Jennifer who was often close to drowning under the weight of heartache about her MS world.

You see, I lived in an almost constant state of terror that MS would show up in my body in terrible ways, overtaking me. Of course, I did not know what that would look like – the range of symptoms offered by MS is considerable and fairly indiscriminate in terms of on whom and how they unleash themselves. All the more reason, therefore, for me to be scared. As well as experiencing the walking challenges of stiffness, a limp, inability to manage any real distance, stand for any length of time, and balance (low heels at work only), were the electric currents I would feel almost without interruption up and down my body. They were not painful but totally freaked me out. Sometimes they were fairly weak in which case I could reasonably concentrate on work. But at other times it was as if I was connected to the National Grid. Randomly and with no warning they would intensify, causing one or both of my legs to jolt.

That was incredibly distracting not to mention embarrassing in front of colleagues. My big fear was that stronger currents combined with weakness in my right leg meant I was getting worse. What if my left leg became weaker too - now named 'the good leg' by me? If that happened, how soon after would I need to use a wheelchair? And what if MS began to affect my arms as well? In fact, if it got to that, meaningful life would surely be at an end with little physical ability to engage.

On and on the tormenting thoughts would go. You get the picture.

With hindsight a big miss was that no medic sat me down in the early stages to tell me what might or might not happen or even what should not cause me alarm. That would have been so helpful. Because no one did, fear roamed freely. I now know, for example, that intense electric currents do not necessarily signal progression but I did not then. While I understand that medics cannot make accurate predictions about MS, the absence of receiving any guidance left an open door to anxiety at its worst, which was not helped by most of the available books on MS at that time being miserably negative. Thankfully it is far better now but there was little optimism to be found in print in those years.

On top of the physical pressures at work, I also needed to build relationships with colleagues. Although they were only welcoming, my world had lost its ease which meant I was often a mix of on-edge, self-conscious, and inhibited around them. The social, carefree Jennifer who dived into making friends at law school twelve months earlier just wasn't there.

And there were challenges meeting clients for the first time. I imagine I presented a confusing picture. On the one hand, a smiling, seemingly healthy young woman, on the other, a fragile figure leaning on a stick to walk. Frequently, they would sympathetically ask what I had done to my leg, probably expecting a twisted ankle story, only to be rather taken aback by my 'it's MS,' answer. Eventually I learned that if an explanation was needed, it was better I offered it before being asked. Like telling a client I would organise a taxi to take us to a meeting nearby 'because with MS I hobble a bit'. I discovered if I exhibited confidence and dismissiveness about my limitations, that set an upbeat tone making it a non-issue for all. Helpful insight on managing MS at work when it finally came, but before it did, yet another pressure in my delicate world of barely getting by.

But in the midst of the challenges, I would not be painting a fair picture if I did not mention some lifelines too. Without question, the outstanding one was my adorable Aunt Freda who met me daily from the train. I owe her so much. Each evening she gave me space to offload my distress at the latest symptoms before my firm announcement I could not face another working day.

In her practical, no-nonsense Irish-way, she ignored my doomsday predictions, offering food instead as the immediate cure with 'Sure have your dinner and we'll see how you feel in the morning.' And despite my protestations, somehow each morning she would get me off to work again having rebalanced the emotional seesaw of my life with her encouragement to try one more time.

Admittedly quite some distance behind Freda in the lifeline league table, was another from her household; Floppy, the family dog. A rather nervous but affectionate collie mix, she was a wonderful source of comfort to me in those early months. In her canine world, of course she did not know I was having a crisis or that there was one. But she did work out I could never get enough of her affectionate attention and, to my delight, gave me lots. I relished it, even if I knew she was more motivated by the treats I gave her than anything else. But the solace she offered was a balm to my soul, thirsty for consolation of any kind. It was not until some years later I found out my secret camaraderie with Floppy was not as secret as I had thought. At a lunch with Freda, she told me it amused her no end to hear me having grown up conversations with Floppy before going to work when no one else was up. Of course, I had no idea anyone was listening. The things we do to survive!

And so life went on, every day feeling like a monumental challenge to be overcome interspersed with moments of respite in domestic life. No one was more surprised than I then when the days began to be weeks and the weeks, months and, despite everything, I was still going to work.

I did not grasp then what I was learning; that I just needed enough for the day. We are often overwhelmed by life because we look at the long haul ahead wondering how we can gather everything we will need for the journey. But we only have the moment we are in and the day in which we live. It follows, therefore, that if we just reach for what we need for the moment, day, for what is right in front of us, we can keep moving. Conversely, if we try to gather what we think we will need for the whole journey, we will not move at all.

But the towering black shadow I could not get away from was not the diagnosis of MS itself, as awful as that was. It was actually the belief that the hopes and dreams I had for my life were now shattered because of it. I was truly devastated.

When the neurologist told me I had MS, it was as if The London Shard collapsed around me leaving my future in ruins. Hope deserted me. Was that an overreaction? I do not think so. The worst MS can bring is pretty awful, the least far less, but no one can predict its path.

I know now that hope is the heartbeat of life, its fuel necessary for us to lean forwards or move towards something. If we do not have hope, we may be alive but we are not living - merely existing. There is a world of difference.

When hope left me, it was like a balloon losing its air in an instant. In the remaining vacuum, aspirations for travelling, writing, and having a family seemed shredded. It was not that I sat down with a list and tore them up. But I knew a measure of good health would almost certainly be necessary for their fulfilment. Instead, I faced a waiting game to see what havoc MS might wreak. Could hope have a place against that backdrop?

Which all led to *the central question* for me. Why had the loving God I believed in not prevented this from happening? Was He not in control of my life?

How on earth had this happened?

5

ARE YOU THERE, GOD?

If God were proud He would hardly have us on such terms: but He is not proud, He stoops to conquer, He will have us even though we have shown that we prefer everything else to Him, and come to Him because there is 'nothing better' now to be had.

C.S. Lewis

By now my relationship with God had taken centre stage in my life. The years in Manchester had seen great growth in that regard. At the Royal Northern Christian Union (CU), I met young people who talked openly about loving God. This was unknown to me in Ireland. In freshers' week, I still recall my surprise at a conversation with a handsome young cellist as I looked at a noticeboard. To my amazement, he enthused about his love for God as if it was not in any way unusual. But to me it certainly was. And when I got involved in the CU, I began to learn so much. For example, I discovered that prayer is talking to God like a friend; that God wants to speak often because He desires relationship with me; that the Bible is an exciting, readable book enabling me to know God more; and that having Christian friends is a necessary, fun part of the Christian life. In fact, I made some of my very best and lasting friendships in those times, as we students pursued getting to know God more deeply alongside our studies. Back injury aside, they were happy years.

So even though my musical dream had been dashed towards the end of that season, I nevertheless believed God had somewhat redeemed the situation by opening the doors of law. I did not understand why things had gone awry, but I still believed God was good and life full of promise. In short, my faith had not been shipwrecked.

However, the advent of the MS diagnosis was entirely different. It came with no upside but was like a silent sledgehammer hitting my life, seemingly innocently at first by not affecting outright destruction. But within it was the horrible threat it would do its worst in time in the cruellest of ways.

I felt utterly let down by God.

When I considered that reality in the context of a God I had believed to be my loving Father, protector, giver of good things, and sovereign in my life, my initial question, 'Where were you when this happened?' quickly turned into an accusation, 'If you really loved me, how could you have allowed this to happen?'

So, there you have it. I was angry with God and blamed Him. Had He been asleep while this disease crept up on me? I had trusted Him with my life and believed the wonderful promises in the Bible about it. Didn't the prophet Jeremiah say God had plans to prosper me giving me a hope and future? Of course, I understood life had its challenges, but I did not expect serious chronic sickness to be one of them.

Only adding fuel to my anger was the sense of loss that aspirations might not be fulfilled with compromised health. And there was confusion too. What about the numerous prophetic words[2] I had received from people pointing to God's exciting purposes for my life - were they still possible?

In my petulance, I reminded God I was only in my twenties in what should have been my prime, getting back on my feet in law after the musical debacle I had been through. To be diagnosed with MS was bad enough. But to be diagnosed with MS on the brink of a new life in law was a double blow. (Cue my obvious whining at God).

In that very angry place then, you might well wonder where or to what I turned for consolation or answers. Paradoxically I will admit, I found myself turning to God. You see, despite my railing and upset at God, my belief in His existence was unshaken, as well as my conviction that to His great cost He sent His Son, Jesus, to die in place of humanity to enable humanity to reconnect with Him. Much to my childish chagrin even, the fact that I was angry with God did not make any of that untrue. So yes, although His love felt more theoretical than actual to me at that point, and part of me wondered if He really was good, I knew there was nowhere else to turn.

That meant lots and lots of private tears in those early weeks, as I unconsolably poured out my pain and anger to God, desperate to hear His voice. I longed for His comfort, His hope, His tangible presence; frankly any kind of touch from Him would have been welcome just to know I was not alone. Because I did feel completely alone.

Once medical appointments were complete in York, I had retreated home to Ireland before the move to London. In saying I felt alone, I should be clear my family was wonderfully supportive. But because I could see how shell-shocked and distraught they were by the diagnosis, I made sure they never saw the worst moments of my distress. Call it the instinct of love. I could not bear to add to their pain by having them see a daughter and sister who was dissolving on the inside. Perhaps it was worse because we were quite a medical family. My sister was by now a doctor which meant she and my parents were acutely aware of what might lie ahead. So I kept a rein on my emotions. Yes, they saw weak moments but not the naked places of pain I reserved for private times. But there, of course, God saw it all.

It was during that visit to Cork that a defining encounter with God took place. The first night home, very deliberately, I had a conversation with Him. It was honest and anguished where I laid my heart bare. It was about my future and health.

I need to preface it by saying I was clear at the time that healing sickness is the desire of God's heart. Jesus demonstrated that over and over in His life by healing everyone who came to Him ill without exception. Not only did He say He came to give life, but also that He came to destroy the works of the devil whose only aim is to 'steal, kill and destroy' (John 10:10). Sickness does all of those things and, for that matter, injury too.

Crucially, I knew it is still God's heart to heal sickness today, whether by natural, medical, miracle means or any combination – God works through them all. Nowhere is that eternal willingness clearer than in the story of the desperate leper who asked Jesus if

He was willing to heal him. Without hesitation, Jesus says He is and does[3]. By then I had also witnessed healing miracles in other people's lives so had seen Jesus' healing power first-hand. I was in no doubt He is the same yesterday, today, and forever[4].

Nevertheless, that night I asked Him to speak directly to me about my health desperate as I was for the reassurance of His voice. In spite of my mixed-up anger towards Him, I knew He would want to offer it as my friend.

I remember the conversation distinctly as I framed my question. I asked God to be clear that His healing would be the removal of MS symptoms and effects from my body, as well as the heart healing of comfort and peace which I knew was always a by-product of relationship with God. For anyone unfamiliar with MS, there is currently no medical cure, only medications which help hold back progression or relieve symptoms.

Having prayed in that vein I went to sleep. As I woke the next morning, the first thing that came into my mind were the words 'Jeremiah 33'. I was startled. There was a weight to it - somehow, it felt like God's voice. But I had never had Bible references come to mind like that before. I was not sure there even was a Jeremiah 33 in the Bible! Could it really be God?

To my amazement, when I dug out my Bible there it was. And not only that, but the chapter also addressed the very questions I had asked. In it, God repeatedly tells the struggling Israelites, ravaged by wars, that He will heal them. He uses two different words for healing – one, for healing which is restorative, body, mind and heart, and the other which is a cure, literally a cure or bandage to the body. I could not believe it.

I was deeply moved by God's care for me, not only in wasting no time answering my question but in so precisely distinguishing the types of healing I specified. Actually, I was a bit blown away that there even was a single passage in the Bible covering both points. This was God highlighting verses to say with pin-point accuracy, 'Jennifer, I am going to heal you in the terms you asked.', effectively speaking through them as His immediate 'now' or 'rhema'[5] word to me. I was beyond encouraged; newly filled with hope, belief I could cope with London, and reassured healing was coming.

In fact, this moment of hearing His voice was to prove a major fountain of hope to me in the future. In subsequent years before I saw obvious healing, I would need to remind myself again and again of God's promise in those verses when tempted to lose heart.

The waiting time, however, painfully exposed the frailty of my professed trust in God. When I saw those closest to me believing resolutely that I would be healed, I felt relatively strong in faith. But I was easily shaken if I came across Christians who did not. There are those who do not believe God heals sickness today apart from medicine and those who believe He does in theory but may waver in the face of serious disease.

Fortunately, my closest friends believed Jesus' heart is always to heal. They were consistently an amazing strength to me supporting and praying for full health. But I soon discovered I had to learn to walk solidly in God myself, able to trust Him without over-relying on the faith of friends. When my trust for healing wobbled as it occasionally did, it forced me back to Him asking if I had correctly understood His heart to heal. The answer has only ever been 'yes'. As a consequence, slowly over time I saw my trust levels change. The more I practiced turning to God and the Bible for encouragement the more I grew in strength and conviction God would be faithful to His promise. Trusting Him for healing became a place of wonderful liberty as I became ferocious and tenacious about believing God regardless of the beliefs of others.

I should be clear however I am not dismissing what the Bible says about the power of two or three people agreeing together in prayer for God to do something. Jesus tells us how important that is. My point is simply that I had to learn to stand on my own two feet in terms of God's promise to me, as well as know how to be vulnerable and reach out to friends when I needed their support. Critical though friendships are, I learned that being unable to trust God without a friend to prop one up is not a healthy place spiritually. As with so many things in the Kingdom of God I had to learn it is 'both, and', and not 'either, or'.

But back to relating to God. Yes, I had taken great comfort from Him speaking to me in Ireland. I knew my angry heart had softened a little towards Him. But that was only the beginning of this new road which required me to lean on Him to a degree I had not before. If I am honest, I did not like it.

Truthfully, once I moved to London, I struggled to consistently hold onto the hope received in Ireland in the face of the overwhelm of day-to-day life with MS. As a result, the path during legal training was massively 'up and down' with only sporadic progress along the way.

Most evenings I would go to my bedroom to spend some time with God. Sometimes I was in major 'self-pity plus angry with God mode', demanding that He speed up whatever He was doing and heal me. Not surprisingly I usually did not hear or sense God with that attitude; just deafening silence. But desperation is often the birthplace of change or, at least, it was in my case. When it peaked, my heart would soften enough to ask God to speak to me however He chose. And it was generally then that I heard Him. Not audibly, not in flashing lights, but gently.

During the Manchester years, I had begun to learn about hearing God's voice which took me considerably beyond my limited experience in Ireland. I discovered His voice is expressed in different ways, through life's multifarious strands, and that God is speaking all the time. Of course, the Bible is a staple source of His voice and heart as the very Word of God. As I began to read it daily, I would notice particular verses seeming to jump off the page to me as if in capitals which was God speaking to me in that moment, His rhema word. Or a fragment of a song would come to mind relevant to my circumstances, words on a street billboard would stand out, I would feel a tangible peace as I prayed about something which whispered, 'don't worry', or a friend would offer an encouraging prophetic word, timely and en pointe, in a way they could not have imagined. The means of Him speaking is endless I discovered.

Perhaps an example from those trainee times is helpful. One day at work, I had what I called a particularly 'bad leg day' - I did not have 'bad hair days' anymore! I barely made it to and from the sandwich shop to get some lunch, agitated by the effort of trying not to fall on the cobbled London streets while also talking to a colleague pretending conversation was easy. It was not. Walking coupled with talking was now an ordeal.

Then later, when I almost overbalanced getting out of a chair at the end of a client meeting, the awkwardness of everyone in the room was palpable as they, all men, hesitated, probably trying to figure whether catching me to prevent a fall was acceptable, or they ought to do nothing in the name of political correctness. And if all that was not enough, the electric currents were ferocious that day.

When I retreated to my room that evening, I felt depressed, struggling hard against the temptation to wallow in self-pity and scream at God about my life. The script would have been,

'Can't you see, God, it's too hard for me at work - when will you intervene?' But before it got to that point, 'Psalm 40' floated across my mind. I could not have told you what it said before I opened it, but when I did and read the first four verses, all became clear.

'I waited patiently for the Lord; and He inclined to me and heard my cry. He brought me up out of the pit of destruction, out of the miry clay, and He set my feet upon a rock making my footsteps firm.

He put a new song in my mouth, a song of praise to our God; Many will see and fear and will trust in the Lord. How blessed is the man who has made the Lord his trust...'

I knew the words were God's voice to me expressed in the Psalm. This was King David pouring out his anguish in a similar place of despair to me, feeling like his wait for God to help was endless. But God hears David's cry and lifts him out of the *'pit of destruction'* setting his feet on firm ground. Not only could I relate to David's feelings, but the image of footsteps being made firm was loaded with meaning for me. To David it may have been a metaphor for things improving in some way whether he was or wasn't literally stuck in mud. But to me it was both a metaphor for heart rescue — clay to rock is a sizable improvement — but also a repeat of the promise to heal me by making my footsteps firm.

Then as I read on, it says God *'put a new song in my mouth, a song of praise to our God'.* Despite the hard journey, God turned David's situation around so he became joyful and He would mine. When I grasped this, the peace and hope of God flooded my heart and I drank in the promise that I would be blessed or thrive if I trusted God. The atmosphere in my room changed — it literally felt like heaven opened around me.

Once again, I was amazed God had spoken so precisely through a passage in the Bible which reflected my mindset in the moment. I was also deeply touched God got my attention to release hope to me when I was in desperate need. It seemed He lived closer to me than I had imagined.

Still, my journey was erratic as a trainee because I allowed myself to be tossed about by different emotions. One was loneliness. There were certainly friends rallying around to support me, trying to soften the MS blow. But a screaming loneliness was always present on the inside. Howsoever the disease progressed, and with the memory of the elderly woman in hospital still vivid in my mind, I knew the journey of progression would be a solitary one if it came. The most a friend could do would be to hold my hand and say 'I'm here' but, of course, in the busyness of life that could not be constant. So, the aloneness of the future felt large and terrifying to me which led to a sense of aloneness in the present. Without intending it, I think part of me withdrew a little from people, perhaps in preparation for the imagined isolation ahead.

Grief was the other. It showed up initially related to what I believed I had lost of my future, and later in the experience of that loss. I remember leaving a neurologist appointment in year two and sitting in a nearby park. The sense of grief hit me from nowhere. I sobbed and sobbed, oblivious to anyone nearby, asking myself how my world had come to this with medical questions about relapses, progression, and muscle spasm. It seemed a volcano of heartbreak erupted. When its force subsided, I composed myself to go back to work, stuffing remaining grief down, although probably the better for releasing what I had. I never knew when it was coming but it revisited often, usually in my unguarded moments when I realised I could not do something healthy Jennifer could.

Looking back, it seems so obviously stupid of me not to have kept turning to God for help as I was always renewed in strength when I did. But the beasts of my paralysing fear and angry insistence God fix something right away which I believed He should have prevented, still roamed in my heart. Sadly, they often roared above my better instinct to reach to God.

I did not see then that He and I were asking each other different questions:

Me: 'When will I be healed so I can start really living?'

God: 'When will you trust me?'

Yet in spite of my attitude, no matter how far or often I fell into misery, God kept coming to rescue me. He was endlessly patient, coming with a sense of His presence and in fresh voice. Really, He was inviting me into a new authenticity of relationship. In my pre-MS life, what I thought was dependence on God was really dependence on me and the sickness-free circumstances of my life, with a nod towards God. But in my weak place, I could not depend on me which exposed the lack of real reliance. When I grasped this, I knew I could not do life without Him. His invitation was for me to bring Him my brokenness so He could re-dig the foundations of our relationship.

Now as I look back, I can see the breath-taking graciousness of a God who welcomes us even when our approach to Him is qualified. He holds us tenderly as we plead for His help even if, at the same time, we are blaming Him for our pain. I often was.

Notes

[2] Prophetic words are words of encouragement from God through Holy Spirit for edification, exhortation, and consolation (1 Corinthians 14:3). The gift of prophecy is described in the Bible (1 Corinthians 12 and 14) and is available to all believers 'for you can all prophesy one by one, so that all may learn and all may be exhorted' (1 Corinthians 14:31). The Bible strongly endorses its use because it is so powerful in building up and strengthening people as God speaks into their lives.

[3] Luke 5:12-13

[4] Hebrews 13:8

[5] 'Rhema' is one of two Greek words used in the Bible for 'word' the other being 'Logos'. Logos refers to the written Word, the Bible, all of which contains Kingdom truth for believers. Rhema refers to the 'freshly spoken' word, heard as if God has breathed on it so that it speaks in a new way now to the hearer. Hearing from God in this way is a part of every believer's relationship with Him if they are open to His voice as He will speak many rhema words to them throughout their lives.

6

MORE LIMPING AND FALLING

The soul becomes dyed with the colour of its thoughts.
Marcus Aurelius

Back to those years as a trainee. Although it had its challenges, I came to realise working life was a Godsend as it created structure and forced some external normality on my life. But away from work things were very different.

As I have described, private times were often unhappy as I processed my heartbreak. Enjoyment or joy was hard to find. I was new to London, had few friends there, and found it difficult to see those I had as I struggled to walk and use trains. As a result, I spent hours on the 'phone to friends seeking comfort in the early months.

Regrettably for them, though they never complained, there was an edge of desperation to those calls. Invariably, the unspoken question was 'Why hasn't this happened to you?' By then, friends featured really large in my collection of life treasures. I knew I was fortunate to have acquired those I had from all my life stages of school, music, faith, and law. Alongside my natural family, they were family to me. But the twist in my life seemed shockingly unfair. We had been walking through life together with similar hopes and dreams, equal I had thought, and at broadly equivalent life stages. Now my path was potentially taking a dramatic turn for the worse, diverging from theirs. I simply couldn't believe it.

At heart, I was afraid they would leave me. Although I am referring to friendships which obviously do not have the commitment of marriage, my fear was that the flow of life would take them elsewhere. Of course, in every sense I wanted them to live life to the full. But I was not prepared for the sense of panic which came that I was facing a lifechanging illness which they were not. I felt separated from them, as if in a boat with an MS label watching them in their label-free boats floating away, enjoying things that seemed out of my reach like adventurous holidays, dating, simple spontaneity, (I was beginning to forget what doing anything without copious planning around mobility was like).

By the way, if this sounds like the script of a self-indulgent victim, I would be the first to agree. But these were my feelings at the time. It was only later I learned to think, believe, and live differently, leaving a victim mindset behind.

A few months into my training it became obvious I should move closer to work for easier travel. Although that meant leaving the security of living with relatives, it was the right step forcing me out of crisis mode to living independently in a flat-share with someone else. The first was not hugely successful, ending after three months and a conversation with my flatmate anxiously talking about the unpredictability of MS. His discomfort about my remaining was so apparent I quickly looked for another flat. But the next was great. My lovely flatmate was entirely comfortable with my situation welcoming me into her beautiful home. And the arrangement sharing a flat also imposed a good measure of discipline on me – I had to reign in my chaotic emotions somewhat so I did not spread misery. And I did; at least outside the privacy of my bedroom.

But the vision I had had of the new life I would build in London as a solicitor fell apart once MS appeared. Yes, I believed my health was going to be restored. But until that happened, life was full of new, unexpected obstacles I did not know how to navigate.

First, there was London social life. I knew I needed to try to create one, so that life was not just about work. But there were unfamiliar barriers. Because walking was so difficult for me, the logistics of getting to a venue, such as cinema or restaurant, and then moving around it often felt like too much. Think stairs and heaving London crowds for someone with problems walking and balancing. Even getting taxis was fraught with angst. There was the pressure of standing trying to hail one without overbalancing and falling. Then when one stopped, I had to move towards it releasing my legs from the grip of stiffness which seized them whenever I had been in one position for even a few minutes. Those first few steps were the scariest; jerky, unstable, I was terrified of falling. Overwhelmingly taxi drivers were kind telling me to take my time, although I still remember the one, (the only one in fact), who barked at me, 'You don't need a taxi, love, you need an ambulance', before driving off. Often it felt like I expended most of my energy just getting somewhere leaving me depleted when I arrived.

It was also stressful emotionally as I tried to pretend socialising was manageable although it generally was not. Picture standing talking to people in a packed wine bar, trying to appear relaxed at the end of a working day when inside you are counting how many seconds you have left until you need to sit down with no seating area in sight. Just to add to the pressure, you know if you do not sit in time, your legs may completely give way. But you keep trying to participate when invited because, otherwise, when will you mix with colleagues and friends?

Another barrier was my newfound 'girl self-esteem' issue. Having to use a walking stick at age twenty-eight killed my sense of attractiveness, leaving me feeling defeminised as a woman. And even when I did not use a stick, explanation to come, my walking was slow, tense for fear of losing my balance, and awkward. Perhaps this was emphasised all the more because my social world was mainly among the twenty-somethings, the young, healthy, and beautiful. I usually felt foolish, as if trying to be part of something, a life, a 'normal', if there is such a thing, which I should accept was not available to me. Inside, I was grief-stricken. This was the stage of life when I hoped to find a relationship leading to marriage. But what man would risk a life with someone saddled with the unpredictability of MS? Or might there be a man who would hear and believe God's promise to heal me or love me enough not to care anyway? Alternatively, was dating off the radar until I was healed? A flavour of my tormenting inner dialogue which hijacked social events if I couldn't shut it down.

And there were also the work social events. The working world loves standing only events so people can circulate. But I learned quickly they did not work for me because I needed to sit after a few minutes. Some kindly person would always come to talk to me, sitting with or leaning down to me so we could speak. But after a bit, the individual would realise they either had to stay with me all evening or leave me on my own to go talk to others. Awkward. Sensing their dilemma, I would urge them to move on, explaining I was just getting my energy back before I would circulate again too, a half-truth. Or if they were too polite to do so, I would make my excuses and leave. This only had to happen a few times for me to begin avoiding these events entirely, but I feared my absence would be a black mark against me in progression at work.

That said, generally I tried not to give in to my limitations and tried to use the walking capacity I had within reason. But from the small things like walking from the office to my car to being sent to court to file documents, the effect of not being able to walk normally was nightmarish. I remember being sent to the Royal Courts of Justice building in London - impressive with its winding staircases and long corridors, but an impossible venue for me. Bless her, but what was the lawyer thinking who sent me there?!

To paint a broader picture, and perhaps give myself some credit, I did try to expand my social world. However, even with the best planning things could go wrong in my world of fragile legs. Before the days of apps and Ubers, rather bravely, I ventured on my own once to a Young Lawyers' event in central London in the hope I might meet some like-minded people. Unfortunately, when I left at 11pm to get a black cab home, there were none to be found.

After walking and searching for perhaps seven minutes, I simply ran out of leg power, forced to sit on the pavement of The Strand as my legs would not hold me up.

What a sight I must have been. A girl smartly dressed in a work suit, sitting on a footpath in central London late at night. In the freezing cold and dark, I remember crying, quietly wondering how circumstances had got me there, berating myself for my foolishness in thinking I could build a life like other people, and being freshly freaked out by how little walking I could manage. In the end, I did find a taxi and get home. But my confidence was sorely knocked. The internal voices were loud, telling me I was an idiot to think I could live like my peers, reinforcing my fear that I was doomed to a shrinking social landscape.

But there was one hugely positive development during this time; I began to drive in London. I had given up trying to use public transport after a few nerve-wracking journeys when I narrowly avoided collisions with zealous travellers. To my delight medics told me there was no reason I could not drive, so I bought myself a Renault Clio I memorably named 'Walter'. After minor adaptations, I learned to drive with my hands as I could not rely on my legs for driving by now.

Of course, driving in London is not for the faint-hearted. But I managed and for that, somewhat reluctantly, I have to admit to being in Rory's debt. Like most Londoners my brother used the tube but, seeing my nervousness at the prospect of London driving he suggested I practise in lighter traffic at night. Even better, he agreed to come with me for the first few attempts, although wrongly claims to this day that he took his life in his hands by doing so. And while I recall several unwarranted moments of him exclaiming, 'Jenn, watch out - you nearly got us killed!' and a crescendo of 'wrong lane - wrong lane - *wrong lane!'*, the journeys did the trick. Before long, I felt at ease driving in London which meant the door to the world, life, and fun was not entirely closed.

Result.

7

DARK AND LIGHT

No pessimist ever discovered the secret of the stars,
or sailed to an uncharted land,
or opened a new doorway for the human spirit.
Helen Keller

The hardest place for me during those early trainee years, however, was in my own head.

I was an emotional yoyo because I made all the wrong choices in my mind. I let negative thinking be a friend to me. If anyone was brave enough to point out positives in my situation, such as that it was great I had a job or that God works all things to His children's good, I would quickly pour cold water on their remarks. In fact, I was pretty determined to stay stuck in a mindset of all the worst attitudes – self-pity, expecting the worst, angry at the world. Need I go on?

And that is a miserable place. Negative thoughts lead straight to an unhappy heart because our thoughts direct our emotions to a large extent. I learned by experience the truth of King Solomon's words, *'For as he thinks within himself, so he is.'* (Proverbs 23:7).

I felt miserable because my thinking darkened my heart, which in turn sapped me of emotional and physical strength. Sometimes I felt so low, I barely made it to work or struggled to function when I did.

In the times I could be lifted out of negative thinking by a brave and skilful friend, I noticed the more I thought and spoke about positive things, the better I felt. I could actually take pleasure in meeting friends or going to the movies. I didn't see it at the time, but it was usually me who sabotaged the good moments by reintroducing the bad. Bottom line, I was still so angry at God I was not prepared to let Him or my friends forget that something awful had happened. I seemed to think if I had too many happy moments, God would not rush to fix things the way I wanted. So foolishly I kept singing from the 'poor me' negative song sheet.

If I had been wiser, I would have known the only safe place mentally and emotionally was in trusting God. It is always the safest place because He is only ever good. No matter my situation, His kindness and desire to redeem would be activated in my life if I would allow it. Yes, I was hurting from a painful life-event. But to my own detriment I was immature, like a sulking child not getting her way. Which meant I continued to wrap negative thinking around me like a blanket, perpetuating the bleak emotional cycle I lived in for those training years.

Thankfully during this time, I found a good church in London to attend. As mixed up as I was in this season, I knew I needed the input of other Christians to have any chance of holding onto God firmly. Of course, He designed it that way. Every believer is a part of His body with Him as the Head. One of the metaphors in the

Bible describes each person as an individual body part with its own distinct function, aka tongue and eyes. But within it is the other truth that the parts are necessarily interdependent. The human body only functions properly when its parts are healthy. If a leg is broken there can be little movement even if everything else is working - the broken area must be given attention to heal. That lesson of interdependence was mine. I was a broken part needing strong believers to love me through my health crisis so I could be rebuilt in hope, trust, and whatever else I was lacking.

The church was a thriving central London church called Holy Trinity Brompton. It was encouraging just to attend their Sunday services, packed as they were with young adults with all the energy and vibrance that brought. But, of course, real relationships had to be formed for it to have meaningful impact which took time. My first step towards that was joining a small homegroup. That was a group of twenty-somethings who met in someone's home twice a month to eat together, read a bit of the Bible, and pray for each other. Our paths just crossed for a season, but I was nevertheless grateful for them and the sense of anchor and safety they provided in the otherwise choppy waters of my life.

But in that time, there were two rather extraordinary occurrences.

The first arose three months into my training when I began to experience blurred vision. The optic nerve became inflamed in both eyes. Not unusual with MS, but really scary especially when told I could not see a neurologist for six months. There was no one to answer my questions. How long would it last? Could it get worse? Was I going to lose my sight, a possibility, I knew, with MS?

Although I was able to see clearly when my eyes focused in one direction, I could not read, use a computer or go out because any movement of the eyeball caused blurred sight and deteriorated balance. Disastrously it seemed, therefore, I had to be signed off work sick only three months into my new job.

In that condition, I remember spending three weeks at my Aunt's home gripped by anxiety about what was happening. Needless to say, there were many anguished conversations with God as I imagined the worst about what the future might hold. But to my great surprise at the end of the third week, I sensed God saying I should go back to work, and that my eyesight would recover when I did. I was stunned – was that really God? I was not at all used to these kinds of instructions from Him requiring bold steps of faith. Was He actually telling me to go to work with blurred eyesight in the belief it would simply disappear when I got there? Yet in spite of my incredulity, the more I pondered it, the more I felt He was.

Nervously, I got the train to work on Monday only to discover when I sat at my desk and looked across the keyboard, that the blurred vision was just as bad as ever. Horrified, I wailed internally at God.

'What a fool I have been! Why did you tell me to come to work with my eyes in this state, when I will only make things worse with my employer having to go home again?' I was afraid the firm would end my training for health reasons; three weeks' absence so early in the job was not a good sign.

Yet I heard God's reply, 'Who are you going to trust, Me or fear? Believe Me *(i.e. have faith in what I said)* and your eyes will settle'. I was thrown; this was not the response I expected. But figuring I had nothing to lose I decided to and stayed.

And seemingly before I knew it, a secretary's voice called, 'Goodnight, see you tomorrow, Duncan'.

It was the end of the day. I had become absorbed in the work I had been given and time, apparently, had flown by. Quickly I looked down at my keyboard, then speedily from left to right to left to right again, then to reading a document beside me followed by a few minutes of typing. With a racing heart, I began to register what had happened. My blurred vision was gone. I could now type, read without difficulty, and had lost all sense of disorientation.

Amazed and very much chastened, I retreated to my room that evening to thank God for an outright miracle. I was astonished. Just as He had said, my eyesight settled back to normal within the day at work. The script I had written in my mind of an imminent end to my training contract had been torn up by heaven it seemed. Yet as I gushed my gratitude to Him, I did not hear Him say, 'I told you so.' Instead, I sensed His whisper of, 'This won't happen again. Believe Me'. And it never has.

The second event occurred three months later at a conference where I played violin in the worship team - I could play comfortably in short bursts. At that point I used a walking stick all the time, but when on stage at the conference, I got a friend to help me to my chair to avoid the self-consciousness of using it. By the third and final day however I was feeling fairly low; despite my high hopes God might heal me at the event, nothing had happened. In my disappointment, therefore, I just wanted to go home. But God was not finished.

As the morning session was closing, the speaker, Marc du Pont, turned towards me on the stage saying he wanted to pray for the girl playing violin. Surprised but pleased, I stood up and heard him begin to pray for my legs, muscles, and nerves before proceeding to prophesy that I would dance like King David did. If you don't know the story, David was famed for his rather wild dancing before God on one occasion (2 Samuel 6:12-14) which, given my circumstances, was quite a statement. Although Marc continued to prophesy, I stopped listening as I became aware of something else happening to my body. In the natural, MS by now had caused my legs to become terribly stiff, as if there were 'clamps' around my knees. But as soon as Marc began to pray, it was as if the clamps fell off and my knees immediately loosened. At the same time, I felt an incredible joy begin to pour out on me like a waterfall causing me to begin jumping on the spot! Not only was exhibitionism in front of 500 plus people not my norm, but because of MS I should not have been able to jump with such poor balance. Astonished by what was happening, I interrupted Marc mid-flow, asking him if he knew I had MS. When he said he did not I remembered my walking stick was not with me on-stage. Meanwhile in the background, I began to hear ripples of excited shouting and clapping from my friends who saw what was happening. I did not quite know what was going on other than that it was wild!

The end of the story is that my legs and balance immediately substantially improved as a result of the prayer although I was not completely healed. God never needs us to pretend something is happening which is not, so as word began to spread that healing was happening, I asked for the microphone to explain. I am not sure how coherent I was in my excitement but I managed to explain that, in just a moment, God had released those clamps and significantly healed my balance. Rightly, that announcement was followed by a great deal of collective cheering in an atmosphere thick with the presence of God. Personally, my joy was beyond full as I drank in the encouragement of those moments. It felt somewhat surreal. Yes, I had seen healing miracles before but never such an immediate and dramatic physical improvement and yet it had just happened to me!

Still, a major test came on my way home when I sensed God tell me not to use my walking stick again. He said I did not need it. As with my eyes, my trust was being tested – would I believe God or not? Being honest, come Monday I had to dig deep for courage to obey. But I did, pushing myself to believe God instead of my fears. And when I did, I was overjoyed to see I could manage without it, the physical improvements from the conference very much enduring. As I went to work, I wondered how I would explain this extraordinary turn of events to colleagues as they had never seen me walk without a stick. To my amazement, none of them said a word or even registered surprise at my ease walking. Perhaps they did not think it was their place to comment or perhaps it demonstrates the miraculous can be hidden in plain sight from those without eyes to see. And while the Jennifer of the time was too shy to tell them what had happened, I did not allow their reaction (or lack thereof) to prevent my basking in joy over the events and most incredible miracle I had seen.

Of course, the big question is why I was not completely healed? After all, if God was going to demonstrate His healing power, which He did, why not complete the task? Honestly, I do not know. But I do know this landmark experience was a game-changer for me. Whatever the extent of the healing, God sent me a loud message that not only was His hand on my life, but that He was a God of miracles who still did extraordinary, impossible things.

I was also deeply moved by the nature of the healing. Remember I said I found using a walking stick defeminising? Because I no longer needed it after the conference, my self-esteem hugely improved. While I now realise my feelings might have had more to do with my own wrong thinking than truth, I nevertheless immediately felt the difference in self-worth, delighted I could shed the MS signpost of a walking aid.

In the bigger scheme of serious health issues, however, I realise the relative vanity of my concern over whether I felt good about using a stick or not is nothing compared to the far greater suffering many endure. In the world of MS alone, I imagine there are many who would be glad to be able to walk, stick or not. So, I do not mean to be insensitive to those realities by making the point that sometimes God can appear to answer prayer for the less important things ahead of the more serious.

I do not have an explanation except to suggest that perhaps He reaches out with the touch we need at the time. But whatever His actions, we know He cares about our concerns, big and small, which on this occasion He showed me in such a personal, meaningful way.

Most importantly, this healing established a whole new level of trust in me in God for my future. It literally blew the roof off any limited expectations of God I might have had only six months after diagnosis. Now no one could persuade me His promise of healing was remote. It was not. I had just experienced healing first-hand and had every reason to expect more in the future, rubber stamped by God's Jeremiah promise of healing to me.

I was grateful beyond words.

8

THINKING BOOTCAMP

*The truth is that our finest moments are most likely to occur when
we are feeling deeply uncomfortable, unhappy, or unfulfilled. For
it is only in such moments, propelled by our discomfort, that we
are likely to step out of our ruts and start searching for different
ways or truer answers.*

M. Scott Peck

It was a beautifully sunny June day in London, the kind which put
a spring in my heart, if not literally my step, as I arrived at work. I
have to admit that London summers are better than Cork. Far less
rain, much more sun, and, when the capital begins to fill with
summer-clad tourists, a signal for it to sing with busy parks,
outdoor theatres, and the South Bank humming with visitors.
Regrettably, the song's sound doesn't quite make its way into my
office, but I still smiled to myself relishing the season change.

On arrival, I made my way to the litigation department. This
was where I was completing my training after stints in other
departments. It was also the month in which we trainees would
learn whether we had got jobs in the firm as qualified solicitors. I

had applied for a job in the business department as a commercial and corporate lawyer to work with Edward Miller, a partner.

Mid-morning, my 'phone rang. As I answered it, I heard, 'Edward would like you to come to see him,' from Vanessa, his secretary.

'Oh...' I replied, immediately feeling nervous. This must be about the job I thought. Was this a good or bad sign? 'Sure, I'll be downstairs to see him right away.' I responded. As I approached the open door of his office, I tried to read the expression on his face but it gave nothing away.

'Hi Edward,' I began hesitantly as I stepped through the doorway.

'Aaah Jennifer, come in!' His strong voice swamped mine although I thought I detected the slightest smile in it. 'I've got something for you.' He handed me an envelope his expression inscrutable.

'Are you going to tell me what it says?' I asked reservedly.

'Why don't you open it and see?' came his non-committal reply.

By now I was certain the letter would confirm whether or not I had got the job. I was tentatively optimistic it would be good news, reckoning most people do not want to deliver bad in person. Nevertheless, there was a slight tremor in my hands as I opened it.

But there it was, the offer of a job. I was delighted. For any trainee that's the prize but, in my health circumstances, cause for particular celebration. Adding to my satisfaction was the knowledge I would be working for one of the best partners in the firm; exacting I knew, but someone who would train me well. If he or the firm had doubts about my health, this was their opportunity to employ someone else. But they had not. And if I was perplexed by the sequence of God's actions in kindly opening the door to a career in law but not yet fully restoring my health, I was still deeply grateful for it.

So here I was, on the cusp of being a proper lawyer two years after diagnosis. Wholly against my expectations, I had managed to qualify. Not only that, but my health had not got worse, I had been offered a job, I was living independently, and had begun to make new friends. It was all far better than I could have imagined two years before.

Yet despite this milestone I still really struggled. Certainly, I was grateful for the partial healing of eighteen months before. But at age thirty, I hated that restricted mobility hugely constrained my life, that my fear of MS spiralling was as consuming as ever, and my sense of optimism for the future erratic at best.

All of which meant I continued living an emotional rollercoaster my first qualification year. The up and down cycles ground on endlessly, like an old steam train doggedly puffing out smoke, my despair, with only intermittent reprieves at station stops when I could find a bit of hope. But the 'hope stops' were always short-lived before it was back onto the train of despair again. It was exhausting.

Perhaps, therefore, it was always just a matter of time before I came to my end. In any event I did, although not after a particular crisis, but when the cumulative effects of the rollercoaster had sufficiently worn me out. That point was the birthplace of real change, distinct from my panicked God-pleas for help in the shock infused trainee years. As honestly as I knew how then, I reached out to God again for help, trying at the same time to lay my persistent anger down. I say trying, because, in ensuing times, my heart was not always in the place of whole-hearted surrender I was aiming at. On occasion, I was still mad at Him, even when I thought I was not. But I knew there was nowhere else to turn, and life was not working as it was.

To paint a picture of that season life appeared to be functioning well enough on the outside as I was able to do my job. But beyond work, life was quiet and lonely. The highlights were attending church and a weekly visit to my brother for a takeaway. Slightly to Rory's alarm I suspect, I used to half-seriously tell him he *was* my social life! But that left the rest of my time for unhelpful introspection.

Eventually I began to see that when my internal eyes or thoughts were on good things and God's life-giving perspective, everything was better – work, social life, emotional life. But when my thoughts were focussed on me, MS, and everything I could not do I crashed into despair. I should have seen it earlier but did not. Or perhaps I didn't want to.

The hard truth was that my own thinking created the rollercoaster. The majority of it was negative. And that indulgence of negative thinking bred negative feeling in my life. Sometimes it was short-lived before something would engage my mind in a more positive direction. But more usually, I would get stuck in dark thinking for days or weeks.

I began to see that the price for stepping into a miserable frame of mind was huge. It only took me ten minutes to become seriously despairing, a hellish place, but from there it could take weeks to find a way back to hope.

And this was my epiphany - that good thinking which fosters good feeling is critical because it determines whether we live in joy or misery.

Once I understood this, I had to make a decision. Would I decide on purpose to think differently because I realised it was a choice? The mental discipline involved would require my commitment. If it did not, I would be doing it already.

I saw three stages in the thinking process:

1. recognising when I was embracing a negative thought;
2. refusing to do so; and
3. replacing it with a healthy thought.

It sounds as easy as A/B/C but, in reality, it is a battle. Ingrained habits resist being broken. In my case, I had developed a strong habit of quickly giving in to negative thoughts since MS showed up. Now I had to form a new one.

I called it my 'Thinking Bootcamp'. At first, it seemed there were hundreds of moments each day inviting me to go down the negative route. Like mornings when I struggled to walk 200 metres from car to office and panic whispered that I was losing my ability to walk. Or evenings out with friends when I lost my balance and fell, with that inner voice mocking my attempts at normal pleasures. I would recoil with embarrassment on the inside.

But no matter how tempting it was to entertain the worst thoughts when these things happened, I knew I had to think differently. That meant finding something to be thankful for despite my embedded default of negativity. With persistence, I made progress; able to see, for instance, that it was huge the firm had found me parking near a London office or that I had friends who thought nothing of my tripping other than wanting to help.

Crucially I also knew there was a far richer level of transformation available to me by bringing God's word to mind. I should explain. Not only is the Bible a revelation of God inspired by Holy Spirit but, in and of itself, it is alive with the person of God, a living weapon:

> 'For the word of God is living and active and sharper than any two-edged sword, and piercing as far as the division of soul and spirit, of both joints and marrow, and able to judge the thoughts and intentions of the heart.'
>
> (Hebrews 4:12)

The Bible tells us there is a battle for our minds by the enemy of God, Satan or the devil, whose ultimate aim is to destroy humanity. He particularly hates God's people, Christians, because they are His representatives on earth. But he also hates all humanity as they are made in God's image and can become part of His family if they choose.

Is there a spiritual battle for our minds? Without question when we consider the challenge living in a peaceful and hopeful state of mind can be or the amount of mental anguish in the world. The devil's tactic is obvious. For Christians, he will war against our minds to prevent us becoming the powerful people we are when we walk closely with God. And for those who are not yet in God's

Kingdom, he also attacks with lies, negatives, and every kind of mental distress as he attempts to destroy humanity by every means.

But I discovered the Bible contains a glorious and clear blueprint for great mental health, revealed long before psychiatric medicine offered its cures. It is nothing less than life-giving direction enabling us, if we apply it, to be the very best version of ourselves.

After telling us not to conform to the patterns of the world, the apostle Paul tells us to be 'transformed' by the 'renewing' of our minds (Romans 12:2), effectively eradicating negative thinking patterns by laying down new truth patterns through scripture and life-giving thoughts. He makes a huge claim, but it is not exaggerated. 'Transformation' here refers to a metamorphic type change of the magnitude of a chrysalis becoming a butterfly; while renewal means a complete change for the better by continuous renewal. The promise, therefore, is that renewing our minds by continually changing our thoughts for the better will bring an astonishing degree of change.

Which begs the question, what are the right thoughts? Here Paul is also clear, giving us two keys. The first he outlines in his letter to the Philippians:

'Finally, brothers and sisters, whatever is true, whatever is noble, whatever is right, whatever is pure, whatever is lovely, whatever is admirable - if anything is excellent or praiseworthy - think about such things.'

(Philippians 4:8 NIV)

In articulating God's heart, I love that Paul reveals that a sound mind is one that contemplates all that is good and beautiful in the broadest sense and not just so-called 'spiritual' things. He urges us to continually think about edifying things, all of which have their origins in God as He is the source of all life. With the net spread so generously wide, that must cover an array of things such as music, a flower, a good book, a successful business venture, a happy family meal, a clever idea, a child falling asleep, a mountain... Not what a rigid religious mindset might have us believe about the pre-occupations of God.

This is even more compelling when we consider Paul wrote these words from prison at the end of a life of immense suffering. Here is a man so well-schooled in thinking life-giving thoughts on purpose, that his mind was not only steady but infused with the joy of heaven despite circumstance.

The second key he writes to believers in Corinth. Paul tells them to take every thought captive and make it obedient to Christ (2 Corinthians 10:5). Forceful language. That means when we have a thought which is not life-giving, we need to replace it with one that is. For example, using my stick I would often feel self-conscious, thinking I looked decrepit or unattractive, and retreat within myself. Nonsense I now know of course.

But applying Paul's instruction, I had to develop zero tolerance for that kind of thinking and quickly replace the lies with God's truths that I am beautiful[6] and His masterpiece[7] no less. The same process of capturing and replacing thoughts I described earlier but now imbued with the very power of God as I wielded the sword of His Word over my thinking. Fascinatingly, recent neuroscience[8] findings actually validate these biblical principles showing how the brain creates healthy neural pathways from right thinking facilitating good mental and physical health, as opposed to pathways from negative thinking which can offer diminished health.

Critically too we need to recognise these verses are commands, not merely suggestions. Every believer must be fastidious about looking after their thinking life if they are to thrive in the area of mental health. But if they do, the promise is of a healthy and happy mind.

Once I had gathered all this truth, I began to apply it to effect change in me. Like going to the gym and training muscles, I needed to train my mind. That meant not only spotting and replacing negative thoughts for positive ones, but intentionally dwelling on good stuff even in daydreaming moments as well as using Bible verses to fill my mind with God thoughts. I even memorised a few for quick recall when unhelpful self-talk threatened.

It is no exaggeration to say the result of these efforts was like using spiritual dynamite! Without fail, repeating scriptures or good thinking to myself or, even better, speaking them out loud would dispel discouragement and make space for God to fill me with good things such as joy, peace, and hope. Like the Bible says, *'Submit therefore to God* (i.e. think His thoughts). *But resist the devil, and he will flee from you* (i.e. reject dark thoughts).' (James 4:7). With practice, I discovered it was true.

Let me be clear, however, that this is much more than the power of positive thinking. Often people have told me the hope and joy they see in me is purely a result of my steely will to think good thoughts. They give me too much credit - I am not that strong! Yes, it is true I have applied discipline to my thought life, but man's positive thinking has its limits.

In relationship with Jesus, however, there are no limits to inner transformation. Something far greater than the force of positive thinking is at work as we apply God's truth in our lives. We absorb the very life of God in the Word of God becoming like Him. We are also plugged into the inexhaustible resources of heaven in Christ who is in us. When I gave Jesus my hopelessness about MS, He not only gave me the true substance of hope which is found in Him, but I became connected to His endless hope supply whatever my need. Being one spirit with Jesus as I am[9], I am literally 'charged by the divine' with access to the mind of Christ[10]. The extent of that charge depends only on how yielded I am to Him, including the renewal of my mind.

Happily, once my thinking changed, my emotions quickly followed. The crazy turbulence of the previous years was giving way to an evenness and peace I had almost forgotten. I began to experience days, even weeks, of stability; I could hardly believe it. But as it became my reality, I began to understand that enduring happiness or wellbeing is primarily generated from the inside and not external circumstances.

Of course, outside circumstances play a part. We are often legitimately distressed by life's dreadful troubles and do right before God to be honest about how we feel. The very fact that the Psalms are in the Bible shows how much God loves us to be real with Him. But even in distressing times I was seeing there is a journey of thinking in God that can lead us through difficulties instead of our being swamped by them.

Once beyond the old place of constant heaviness, I received an unexpected rather painful insight. That was that the way I had previously lived had established a shallow connection with Jesus. Other than running to Him for help when in need there was little interaction between us. However, it was friendship He desired – He made that clear when He called His disciples friends, not servants. Sadly, I had been stuck in this shallow relatedness for some time. In His love, Jesus always responded to my rescue cries. But it was not real relationship and far less than He offered.

I wonder how many of us live at this immature level where our relationship with Jesus, if we have one, revolves around us asking for help when we need it, but little else? How that must wound Him because He died for us, not only to have eternal connection with Him, but so we can begin as intimate a relationship with Him now as we are prepared to seek. Is that really true? Yes, when we consider He urged us to remain in life-union with Him just as He does with us[11]. What an invitation from the God of the universe.

When I understood this, it changed me. I was saddened and shamed by the poverty of my relatedness to Him. I know we cannot manufacture love – we love Him because He first loved us (1 John 4:19). But as I told Him I wanted to really know and be known by Him instead of merely using Him, I saw a new passion grow in me to pursue Him from a heart of deeper love. I was captivated by the promise of such closeness – how had I not seen it before?

That was when He began to take centre stage in my life in a new way. I would relish time in His presence, often rushing home from work eager to give Him my undivided attention. I would also try to be more conscious of Him throughout my day, by, for example, putting a daily post-it-note with a verse on my desk so I could absorb one of His promises when I looked up from dry legal papers.

In that mindset then, I decided to go on the offensive! Friday nights were evenings that felt particularly desolate. Friends would arrange to meet in London at the end of the working week, but generally I did not join in as my mobility restrictions got in the way. After months of depressing Friday evenings which set an unhelpful tone for the weekend, I decided I was going to make them into joyful times with God. But more than that, this would be a time to foster real friendship with Him – allowing myself to be known by Him while pursuing a deepening love on my part for Him.

At first, it seemed a bit contrived. I felt a tad foolish as I sat down at the piano in my flat to spend time with Jesus playing worship songs. In my mind, I reckoned an evening was two hours but, when it came to it, I wondered how on earth I would fill the time after thirty minutes. The first few Fridays admittedly were somewhat haphazard; a bit of singing, a bit of talking at God, a lot of distraction and wandering mind, and a bit of reading the Bible. But after a few months I knew real change was happening as I went from subdued at the outset to joyful hours later having lost track of time.

My only rule was that I take my eyes off MS and everything negative. And as I did that, I was encountering the One who is full of life, dripping with promise and love. It was reciprocal relationship – me talking to Him, Him talking back to me. Sometimes, for example, He would highlight something to me in His Word, I would chew on it for a bit, and then worship around that theme as He impressed its truth on me. As strange as it sounds, I routinely felt as if my heart had a meal of heavenly gourmet food. And my trust levels grew. Increasingly, I knew Jesus' love for me in my heart as opposed to it just being knowledge. And as life moved on, I was far slower in turning to anger or despair when things did not go my way as I learned to trust Him with the bigger picture.

Which led to another insight. That is that one small decision can lead to enormous change.

The alteration to Friday night meant the whole weekend was better. That, in turn, affected the following week at work when my tank was full of a happy heart after a weekend close to Him. My weekday evenings of complaint to God were being replaced with a heart established on Friday's joy. For the first time, I understood what the writer of Psalm 84 meant when he wrote about going from '..strength to strength..' in the valley of Baca or trouble. In my valley of trouble, through fixing my eyes on Him instead of my problems, I was not only growing and changing in friendship with Him, but now passionately in love with Him too.

And for anyone surprised by talk of passionately loving Jesus, you only need to read Song of Songs in the Bible to catch a glimpse of the bride/bridegroom relationship we are invited into as much as friendship. It was only later I realised my pursuit of Jesus on those Fridays began something; a more intimate knowing of Him and desire for that above all else in life, which only grew and bore fruit in later years.

Once I saw the change arising out of Fridays, the worst time in my week becoming the best, I knew I needed to apply the same mindset to other situations. For example, pre-MS I loved to go walking with friends in parks but, with MS, I could not (and would not countenance using a wheelchair at that point). In the early MS days, there had been times I would insist friends go without me, reassuring them I would be happy sitting in a café. Being honest, the first few times they did I fought back tears when they left, the sadness I could not go with them hitting me sharply as I absorbed my reality, painful even if I knew healing was on its way. However, as I began to focus on being thankful for all that was good especially in restricted circumstances, I began to see upside in almost every setting - welcome 'me time' alone in a café with a book, enjoyment of the view on a park bench while friends were walking, or delightful chats with strangers offering to help if I walked stiffly. In my 'Thinking Bootcamp' mode, I practised refusing to give attention to the bad or difficult and it worked. I did not feel miserable - I was joyful!

If I had to describe this season in one sentence, it would be that I set about changing my mind which changed my heart which then changed my world.

When I did, I discovered that by letting God fully into my life with its disappointments, He changed me for the better teaching me His ways.

It was as if bitter things were not without sweetness. There was blooming even in desolation. As I permitted His touch, I was learning how not to allow disease rob me of the present or hope for the future.

MS ceased to be command and control in my life, Jesus was. A seismic shift for me, a huge triumph.

Notes

6 Song of Songs 4:1-2

7 Ephesians 2:10

8 Dr Caroline Leaf, Switch on Your Brain: The Key to Peak Happiness, Thinking, and Health

9 1 Corinthians 6:17 *But the one who joins himself to the Lord is one spirit with Him.*

10 1 Corinthians 2:16 *But we have the mind of Christ.*

11 *"So you must remain in life-union with me, for I remain in life-union with you. For as a branch severed from the vine will not bear fruit, so your life will be fruitless unless you live your life intimately joined to mine."* John 15:4 TPT

9

FORWARDS

Whatever you do you have to keep moving forward.
Martin Luther King

'Hallo, are you Jennifer?' the gentleman enquired in a marked German accent as he approached me in the lobby. He was tall with a slender frame, probably around forty, younger than I had thought.

'Yes, you must be Peter.' I replied, as I stood up, extending my arm to his handshake. So, this was the German lawyer I had been speaking to in recent months; we were finally meeting in a hotel in Munich. Immediate impressions were good. His warm smile suggested he was as amiable in person as on our 'calls. I felt relieved; this boded well for the next few days.

'Flight ok? My car is outside – just twenty minutes to the office.' he went on in perfect English. And with that I followed him, continuing in easy conversation.

Now in my early thirties, this trip is one of my fondest memories as a young lawyer. I was two years qualified and working on a case with a German client in an area of law I loved;

competition law. Edward had asked me to spend some time at their base in Munich so we could better understand their business, which meant I was dispatched for a few days of meetings with Peter and other managers. I enjoyed it. It was satisfying gathering information, building trust with people in the business, and experiencing a bit of the city when we went out to eat.

Had the workplace pressures of dealing with MS disappeared? Regrettably not; I was always nervous about managing trips away from the office. I told Peter in advance I could not walk long distances, but not that I had MS as I did not want him to make assumptions about my health before meeting me. By then I had found that people often did, more out of lack of knowledge than ill-will. Because Peter and I had worked really well together until that point, I decided if my restrictions needed to be mentioned I would prefer to do so in person. As it happened, they did when I began to struggle walking on the factory tour. Peter kindly immediately ended the tour when I explained, although I noted the sad expression on his face.

I found myself wanting to reassure him I would be okay as I would be healed. But being in work mode and more reticent in those days, I did not. Instead, I smiled, saying it wasn't a big deal before changing the subject. Rightly, it barely featured in our conversation again and, much to my relief, the visit ended well. But every trip brought huge anxiety about how I would manage physically; draining to say the least.

Putting aside the shadow of MS, these were good years as a junior lawyer. Now past the awkwardness of traineeship, I was growing in confidence, appreciating law's challenges, as well as the varied people interaction it brought. And I very much enjoyed working with Edward, learning and valuing the increased responsibility he allowed me over time.

A part of the job I was not expecting, however, was periodically giving presentations to clients. At first, I was aghast at the prospect. I had all but forgotten my school day forays into the world of public speaking or that I had enjoyed them. But once I got over my initial fright, I rediscovered it as a place of ease and confidence for me. In fact, despite 'fragile MS legs', oddly I always preferred to stand rather than sit when presenting. And when I did, my legs were always strong enough. Perhaps the power of doing things we enjoy?

But as much as the work was satisfying, it was also demanding. My lawyer colleagues and I worked extremely hard, a well-known feature of London City law-firm culture. By that I mean that a good day was 8am – 7pm but often did not finish until 8 or 9pm which, stating the obvious, leaves little mental downtime outside work in a day. On top of that, there were the frequent deadline driven projects which kept us at work well into the early hours and occasionally all night. It was intense and hardly conducive to balanced living. But among City firms, mine was known for its more reasonable lawyer expectations, which meant that colleagues were not oblivious to the pressures when work demands ratcheted up. In fact, it was the notable camaraderie within the firm which made the intense times tolerable.

Remarkably too, I had plenty of energy for the pace of work despite debilitating fatigue being a common MS symptom. Initially, I worried that fatigue or other symptoms might be triggered by the demands of the job. But with no apparent ill-effect in the first year, I relaxed, reasoning that as God had given me the opportunity, I could trust it would not cause me harm. Time proved me right as the intensity of work never did adversely affect me to the surprised comment even of my medics. And while I noted the irony that it was sometimes me who stayed late at work, sending tired junior colleagues home, I was still enormously grateful I was managing so well.

Thankfully work was not all serious either, with memorable moments of fun among the lawyers. On one occasion I remember losing a piece of stationary, a metal spike attached to a piece of wood used to collect paper notes - rather lethal but effective. After a bit of searching and not finding, I forgot about it. However, three weeks later, I happened to lean back in my chair only to see the spike hanging from the ceiling above my head! Guessing who the culprits were, I challenged Mark and Simon particularly citing the obvious dangers of a spike hanging directly above me. But while they made a feeble attempt at an apology, I noticed they could barely contain their amusement. When I, rather irritated, pressed them to tell me what was so funny, they told me they had bet I would discover the spike within two weeks but couldn't believe it had taken me three, at which point they burst out laughing again. Hard perhaps to imagine that they were serious and capable lawyers when they needed to be, but I admit a great source of fun in the midst of stressful jobs!

Aside from work, life in my thirties moved on at quite a speed. In the early part, I bought a flat in London upgrading to a house a few years later. It was a sensible investment and, initially, a big move living on my own. But in time it became a welcome sanctuary to recharge from my busy working life. By now my siblings were married, so nephews and nieces began to arrive - five boys and two girls. I loved being an auntie and took every opportunity to be involved with the children as they grew up. When they asked about my unsteady walking, I used to tell them I had a 'wobbly leg' which was going to get better because God had told me it would. Just as only children do, they accepted my explanation unquestioningly, often sweetly trying to help me. Interesting holding the hand of a wriggling five-year-old, who thinks he's helping you walk, when you are already a bit unbalanced!

In this season, I also began to make friendships in London, some of whom are among my dearest today. My first new friends were a couple with two young boys, Debs and Nick. We met through church and discovered we lived close to each other which meant that, to my delight, I had some friends I could visit without the barriers of taxis, cost, and detailed planning. And not only had I found people with whom I could enjoy conversation and shared faith, but I loved that they drew me into their family life as well as fun times with their boys. Gradually, there were other friends too who wonderfully insisted I join in activities which I would otherwise have disqualified myself from. I had learned by then that exclusion, and the isolation it brings, is a big consequence of disability so my friends' tenacity in making sure I participated was treasure.

Even then, I could see that God brought the very best people into my life.

Church life also improved. I found new things to get involved in such as young adult events or courses. Often, they were only for weeks or months here and there, but it all enabled social contact which was a life-line even if fleeting.

And within that mix of activities, I found a new space to grow the prophetic gift I had. During my Manchester years, I had seen its beginnings as I learned to hear God and prophesy over people, articulating the encouraging things He wanted to say to them. I had also known the powerful impact of receiving prophecy myself; the comfort and inspiration released by an accurate word from someone speaking to issues they knew nothing about in my life. I realised a word from God was a lighthouse in the middle of difficulty. More than once, it had been for me.

But absorbed and shocked as I was coping with MS and my job, I had put the gift away for a time. However, once settled at church, I could not help but find myself hearing God's voice afresh, nudging me to offer prophetic words to people in my path. So I did, flexing my spiritual muscles to listen and getting involved in groups that were teaching how to hear God's voice. Bit by bit the gift grew in use and acknowledgement by those around me until I recognised that God's call on my life in this area was strong. To the extent I could, I tried to learn although probably did not quite find the measure of training I was looking for. But I had learned by now it was better I trust God and step into whatever opportunities He presented than sit on the side-lines and complain.

Another gift which saw fledgling expression and growth around that time was preaching. After being asked to give a few talks to mid-size groups at my church, I recognised my huge passion for communication in general, and in particular, preaching the voice and heart of God. Without question, it was where I was most fully alive, competent, and free.

Of course, this was alongside my day job as a lawyer in that decade, but I nevertheless strongly recognised that God's deepest call on my life was to speak for Him. Quite how that would unfold I did not know, but I increasingly knew being a lawyer was an interim role on the path to being a bold advocate for the voice of God.

Anyone who has lived through their 30s will know it is a distinctive decade in some regards. What I mean is this. If you have met your life partner or are married by your 30s, you may be happily on the way toward the domestic life you want. But if that is your vision and you do not yet have it, or at least the partner, nagging worries can creep in that you will not meet someone and will miss out on the life you hope for. Of course, the angst of that in-between life stage was not unique to my generation, although that decade did see new conversation around those questions.

Perhaps the changed tone of the times and dilemma of many thirty-somethings was captured in the romantic comedy, 'Bridget Jones's Diary', coincidentally released in my thirties. Not only could I relate to the 'woman who wants to be married but isn't yet' sensitivity, I also wrestled with the fear 'Is MS a barrier to me having any of that?'

Admittedly that was at odds with my belief by then that marriage was something in God's heart for my life. On the occasions I had talked to God about it before my diagnosis, I had felt His 'yes'. And when I asked the marriage question again, albeit shell-shocked after the diagnosis, the sense was the same. Nevertheless, unsettling doubts often pushed their way into my thinking that it would or could happen. Therefore, in that decade of friends dating, getting engaged, and married, my heart often lurched between fear of lifelong singleness and anticipation of married fulfilment.

The deep trust I knew I should have in what God had spoken, did not always feature. Not the same tumultuous issue as dealing with a serious health condition but nevertheless difficult and painful in its own way.

10

HOPE

Tribulation worketh impatience, and impatience misses the fruit of experience, and sours into hopelessness...
But what a wonderful alteration takes place when the heart is renewed by the Holy Spirit!

Charles Spurgeon

Despite trying to live my thirties well, too often it felt like living on a tightrope.

If I walked with my eyes on Jesus, I stayed on the tightrope. But if I looked away, comparing my life to friends or focussing on health, I fell off in despair. In spite of knowing how to keep my mind and heart healthy, I did not. Worse still, I knew this was not the abundant life God wanted me to live. Surely there had to be a place I could be anchored in Him so I did not keep falling into darkness. And that is what pushed me to an exploration of hope.

My first discovery was that for lasting transformation I needed to live continually in God. This was very different to me living from intermittent encounters with God. Only a constant connection would yield the heart stability I craved, and free me from my erratic pattern.

I also knew I had to begin living in a much deeper daily hope so I could stay rooted in it. After all, hopelessness was my primary battleground.

I understood the more fleeting hope encounters I experienced from my Word and worship times would no longer do. I could not seem to hold onto hope from them. No, I was intent on pursuing something far greater, a residing of hope within me to transform my soul. The Bible explains hope's affects best:

> 'This hope we have as an anchor of the soul, a hope both sure and reliable and one which enters within the veil...'
> (Hebrews 6:19)

The metaphor speaks volumes. Hope is an anchor and anchors have weight. They hold things in place like a boat unable to drift at sea once its anchor is dropped. Hope does the very same for our souls, preventing the mind, will, and emotions wandering and derailing us.

Faithful as He always is, once I began asking God the 'how to inhabit hope' question, I started to find answers in His Word.

First, I saw that our true hope is the promise of eternal life with God in a perfection of love we can scarcely imagine beginning now in relationship with Jesus. When we invite Him into our lives, He comes to live in us becoming our gateway to eternal hope.

> 'Christ in you the hope of glory' (Colossians 1:27)

But there is also hope in the here and now - it is the joyful, positive expectation of events happening or circumstances changing for the good. If you do not think of hope in quite those terms, imagine now anything you hope for or desire and you will find you are aiming towards something better, different or more than you currently have; it affects positive expectation.

Hope is always rooted in God because all goodness flows from Him. This is true for people whether they know God or not; hope does not exist apart from Him. He is its source and creator. As Jesus is the fullness of God, He is the fullness of hope. Therefore, if we know Jesus deeply today, we can know fullness of hope today.

For me this discovery was the most enormous relief. I realised hope is not in trying to get something from Jesus, but is to be found in union with Him, the one who is perfect hope and love. Seeing that was the necessary precursor to pursuing Him to experience it. Just a little perspective shift can change so much.

However, a bigger discovery was that the depths of hope I was seeking were formed only by a very particular journey. It is described in Romans 5:2-5:

'...... and we exult in hope of the glory of God. And not only this, but we also exult in our tribulations, knowing that tribulation brings about perseverance and perseverance, proven character; and proven character, hope; and hope does not disappoint, because the love of God has been poured out within our hearts through Holy Spirit who was given to us,'

As Paul writes about exulting in hope of the glory of God, he sets an exciting tone. But as we read on there is no sugar-coating the process - real hope is carved out of trial. At first, I was utterly dismayed - I did not want to consider that the pathway to hope might involve hardship. I had had more than my fill of that. But reflection brought sense. If God was good then it must be the case that all His pathways were good too. I cautiously resolved to explore further.

I read on. Paul says we are to rejoice in trials knowing that develops perseverance, which in turn develops good character, which then produces true hope. True hope has a priceless substance coming, as it does, from a journey of trusting in God and His goodness through the fire of processes of life we would generally rather not face. They are progressive stages of growth, each building on the one before. But when we arrive at true hope, we are assured it will not disappoint because we already know God's love which contains hope having had to dig deep for it on the difficult journey.

In the Bible, James even confirms the importance of this journey when he says when endurance (or perseverance) is fully developed we will be perfect and complete. And this is not a one-off event. Paul is saying this cycle towards hope will be repeated in different trials in our lives. Then our hearts will become so dyed in hope's ink that it will become ingrained in us.

When I saw God's pattern for forging hope, I understood it generally does not become deeply rooted in us when life is easy, because life pleasures provide sufficient supply. But adversity exposes its shallow roots, as MS did in me. When circumstances did not provide me with reason to hope, I then had to find it in God.

Jesus points to this in the parable of the sower describing the seed which never bears fruit in hearts, as being choked by the cares of life. These are the people who, in the face of worries, do not dig deep into His hope when their own resources run out.

As I studied further, I learned that tribulation refers to 'pressure, affliction, distress' and not sickness per se. Yet my struggles with MS ticked all those boxes. **That meant I had begun a journey which could lead me to hope if I was willing. But willingness is crucial.**

I could choose to remain bitter about the challenges I faced and never get to true hope if I resisted at any stage of its formation. My flesh, or sinful nature, preferred gratification and quick fixes. But to live in a constancy of hope, I needed to have surrendered to it all. God is gentleman enough to allow me the choice.

Alongside this understanding, God began to teach me about the misplacement of hope. I was familiar with God's promise that if we delight in Him, He will give us our hearts' desires (Psalm 37:4). I had often heard people quote and teach on that verse. But God corrected my understanding. Hope is not pre-eminently a belief that God will fulfil desires in our lives, as exciting and hope-inducing as that thought is. Hope is in the person of Jesus. When our hope shifts to fulfilment of desires more than Him, we actually step away from true hope. To my detriment I made that mistake many times.

There is critical divine order in God's instructions. First, we must delight ourselves in God and then from that place fulfilment of our desire will come. But if our primary focus is on our desire that becomes an idol, i.e. something we put ahead of Jesus.

Do not get me wrong - the fulfilment of dreams and desires is necessary for true life. God gives us desires He longs us to fulfil having created us out of His own dreaming. As King Solomon said, *'Hope deferred makes the heart sick, **but desire fulfilled is a tree of life**'* (Proverbs 13:12 emphasis added). We flourish when we live out our desires because, in doing so, we activate the DNA of heaven God placed in us. But they are not the end in themselves; connection with Jesus is.

I learned over time that misplaced hope is very costly. I have known Christians who really loved God but had their worlds fall apart in these circumstances. They became crippled with disappointment at the seeming delay in fulfilment of desire as their hope was fixed on an event instead of a relationship. That relationship with Jesus places hope deep inside us, regardless of events. A subtle but huge difference.

This was a major lesson because it was the very mistake I made for years which led to a bumpy road. Without realising, I had placed my hope almost entirely in the promise of healing, rather than Jesus Himself. Therefore, when it did not materialise in my timeframe, my tendency was to fall into disappointment and anger. I missed that the person of Jesus **was** my hope, which meant if I kept my eyes fixed on Him, I would know the safety of trust and hope in God rather than circumstances.

I learned hope also serves us well while we wait for desires to be fulfilled. Paul tells us that if we hope for the things we do not yet see, our hearts will eagerly wait for them with perseverance.

Therefore, this is not a languishing heart posture but one of anticipation! Eugene Peterson puts it masterfully when he says:

'...That is why waiting does not diminish us, any more than waiting diminishes a pregnant mother. We are enlarged in the waiting. We, of course, don't see what is enlarging us. But the longer we wait, the larger we become, and the more joyful our expectancy.' (Romans 8:24-25 TM)

And even the waiting serves great purpose. From receiving a promise, to the fulfilment of it, there is a necessary process of preparation and testing which means dreams may not come as quickly as we would like. Moses, for instance, spent forty years in the desert while God dealt with his heart. I was no different of course (though a little faster than Moses!) and saw God refining my own heart as I waited for promises to be fulfilled. At times I allowed frustration and discouragement to get the better of me, complaining to God about the waiting.

But as I slowly began to grasp that my resting place in waiting was hope in Jesus, I saw it was my opportunity to grow well. The longer I took to mature and grow well, the longer the waiting would be. God will not rush to take us to our destination if we have not completed the training. Proof of that was the complaining Israelites' forty-year journey in the desert instead of just eleven days. Far from waiting being a negative experience, a common perception in our speed driven society, it is a place of excitement and growth.

This was a WOW moment for me when I understood it.

I discovered too that the most dangerous tripwire to living in hope is disappointment. Of course, it is not wrong to feel disappointed, but the painful, even crushing feelings which can result from it need to be brought to God to be healed. If they are not and we surrender to their effects, our hearts become poisoned with negative emotions. Often, we bury disappointments, in denial that they are heavy rocks in our hearts. During a large part of my thirties, I was quietly angry at God and His apparent delay at doing the things I wanted Him to do, like heal me and bring marriage into my life. But because I was not entirely aware of it, I pushed my disappointments down. What I did not understand, however, was that disappointment took up space in my heart which limited the space for hope. When I eventually gave up my anger towards God, the exchange was glorious - I received lightness of heart instead of gloom. What a huge relief!

But there was a final discovery about hope that came later. I found it in a rock bottom moment around eight years into my thirties.

I vividly remember the evening. It was one of deepest despair when I did not feel I could bear the continued struggle with my restricted life. I cannot remember what led me to that point but do recall feeling horribly hopeless. It was then I stumbled across a talk online by David Hogan, an American missionary to Mexico and modern-day General in God's army.

He spoke about hope and how he had learned to refuse to go through the doors of despair and hopelessness in his heart. Because I knew that the circumstances he faced in life were far worse than mine - persecution in Mexico on a scale I could not conceive of - he had my attention. Interesting, isn't it, how something spoken at the right time can be like a branding iron on one's heart that changes everything? That was how it was for me. As I listened, a picture came to mind of a row of doors all with different names such as sadness, self-pity, despair. They say a picture paints a thousand words. In spite of all I thought I had learned by then, in that moment I saw that I still periodically went through these doors when God did not do things my way.

Then came a new jewel of understanding as David unpacked Romans 15:13 - the measure of hope God wants us to have.

*'Now may the God of hope fill you with **all** joy and peace in believing, so that you will **abound** in hope by the power of Holy Spirit.'* (Romans 15:13 emphasis added)

It was as if I read these words for the first time. Not only does God explicitly link His nature to hope, as 'the God of hope', but He wants me to 'abound in hope'. The word for 'abound' can also be translated 'bubble up' or 'overflow'. This is extravagant language. Paul is saying that unlimited hope is available and the verse explains how I can get it. God will fill me with joy and peace as I believe (some translations say 'trust') Him, which will cause overflowing hope to be released by the power of Holy Spirit.

The impact of my understanding this was huge. In addition to now knowing that real hope was first in God Himself, I was gripped by the knowledge I could receive overflowing hope. That evening

I revelled in this truth and literally felt the pool of darkness I was in drain away as I set my hope on God the hope-giver.

Whatever my thinking was to that point, it changed that evening. I resolved to aim not to go through negative doors again but to open wide the door to the truth about hope. This new insight was akin to receiving a powerful new weapon in the battle for hope. And it would be true to say it changed my path thereafter. It took intentionality on my part to say 'yes' to hope being formed in me, but I was now quicker to embrace the journey of necessary testing to lead me to it, buoyed by the knowledge that boundless supply of hope was available.

I looked less to finding a moment of encouragement from a worshipful atmosphere or talk, valuable though they are, and more to appreciating that the tough moments lived with a great attitude, thankfulness, and trust in the God of hope were taking me on a direct road to overflowing hope.

And to what effect? As hope became more established in me, I changed. Yes, I was more hopeful but it was so much more. I became aware of deep reservoirs of life-giving hope in me, that were always pointing me to Jesus and to a pursuit of greater supply.

Honestly, hope feels like a volcano in my life. Its power is not always on wild display in my demeanour but it is constantly simmering if not boiling on the inside, close to eruption when hopelessness threatens. And all this with the strong assurance I can access whatever I may need for whatever I may face.

I recognised too that hope releases and infuses enormous strength. Even in bad times a flicker of hope was enough for me to feel I could face anything; to move forwards and upwards. It is the heartbeat of heaven which only increased the closer I got to God in difficulty. I saw the hope-filled me affecting those around me.

Paradoxically when my health got worse, people seemed to gravitate more towards me as if wanting to draw from my new marriage to hope. I could feel it. And then I began to understand why those who have the most hope are said to have the greatest influence. Hope contains life. It emits the pure light of heaven and, whether people realise that or not, they are attracted to it.

But I was rather amazed to realise it was largely the pressure and squeeze of MS in my life that enabled God to fashion hope in it. That seeming contradiction of bad yielding good although I was beginning to recognise the ways of God in these patterns. The triumph of sweetness over bitterness.

Of course, the journey is ongoing. I am jealous for the quantum of hope I know I do not yet walk in. But because I now recognise that boundless supply is available, I am compelled to pursue God for it. His invitation shouts loud to those who love Him, to reach for it, especially when we see the scale of hopelessness in the world. But God has all the hope supply needed by mankind.

In light of that staggering truth, here's a question. Could we as believers, access the measure of hope which will eradicate poverty or depression or drought? Or is that even an intelligible question?

We know that God will reward earnest seeking. Therefore, why should it not be me, or you, who seek to become hope carriers to a degree the world has never seen; releasing more of heaven than we can imagine, wreaking havoc on the work of the enemy? Is it not time to pursue the measure of hope which will bring real change to the world? Is God actually looking and waiting for the most audacious dreamers?

11

STRETCHING

Comfort is your biggest trap and coming out of comfort zone your biggest challenge.
Manoj Arora

As time moved on, I found myself in a new job entering a different world. Although I had been happy in my law-firm, in my late thirties an opportunity came my way to work as a company lawyer. When I was first approached about the role, my instinct was to say no as a move had not been on my radar. But when I talked to God about it, I was surprised by a sense it was right. It would be a promotion for me as Head of Legal & Human Resources (HR) and a stretch as I had no experience of HR. But with the company convinced I was right for the job, I decided to make the move.

Because it was a financial services company, I was thrown immediately into a world of traders and brokers. However, I settled quickly, welcoming engagement in the business, the demands of a senior position, and the opportunity to shape culture. It was busy, fast paced, and occasionally uncomfortable - after all who likes firing people - but I appreciated the new mix of law with HR.

Alongside the steep learning curve of the role, I found God stretching me in other ways. By now, I was going deeper and steadier in my walk with Him, better anchored in hope. But from that place He began to push me out of my comfort zone. What I mean is that not only would I hear Him speak to me about other people, but in the most unexpected situations He would nudge me to tell them what He said. That was anytime, anywhere, not just in Church! At first, I was rather terrified at the prospect. What if they were hostile or shouted at me? On the other hand, if what God had to say was important for their lives, shouldn't I take the risk? So very tentatively, and not before I'd bottled out of a few opportunities, I began to obey God with rather wonderful results.

One story stands out in my memory. It was close to Christmas when I found myself in a London airport due to fly to Scotland for the company's Christmas weekend. Reading in a café, I sat on a high stool barely aware of people coming and going around me. Eventually I was interrupted by a guy about my age tapping me on the shoulder to ask if the seat beside me was free. Having replied yes, I turned back to my book to continue reading. Somewhat to my dismay however, I immediately felt a familiar feeling, that internal 'stirring' I recognised as God pressing me to speak to this man.

'Oh no,' was my honest initial reaction. After a minute telling myself I was imagining it, I gave up my attempts to read as I could not concentrate. I might as well give in I told myself and ask God what He wanted to say. So I did.

Straightaway, an unusual picture dropped into my mind. Experience has taught me that if I take a moment with God asking

Him what He is saying, clarity will come. After all, if He wants me to speak to someone, I need to know what the message is. Once I did, I knew I had to find my courage quickly and talk to him in case he left for his flight. So, somewhat with my heart in my mouth, I turned to him, asking if I could interrupt. He had a warm face and, although obviously surprised by the approach, nodded his agreement.

'My name is Jennifer. I'm a Christian and believe in Jesus.' I began. 'I know this may be unusual to you but sometimes God speaks to me about other people. And He wants me to tell you something encouraging. Would you like to hear?' Sadly, I have found that most people have a harsh view of God expecting Him to say condemning things, which is why they are often only open to hearing if I have told them the message is encouraging. Although I saw some confusion on his face, I sensed his curiosity as he nodded yes.

I then began to describe the sequence of pictures or vision I had seen. I told him I saw him walking around a very large black box situated in the middle of a road. In some desperation, he tried to move it but could not as it was so heavy; immovable in fact. He kept trying, looking increasingly distressed as he did, until he grasped he was powerless over it. I could sense the horrible darkness the box emitted in his life. However, as the vision developed the atmosphere and scene began to change as I saw him striding past the box dressed in sports gear running ahead full of life. I described what I had seen explaining God was saying he was deeply troubled about something in his life which he could not shift or resolve. But the scene in which he was running in different clothes past the box was God saying there was hope and a future for him past it where he would thrive.

'Does that make any sense to you?' I finished waiting for his response.

'I don't believe in God but...' he faltered as his eyes welled up with tears. 'But that's incredible. You have exactly described what is going on in my life right now. I can't see any way forward.' he continued. I felt a well of compassion for him, sensing his huge distress.

I replied, 'I have been sitting here for thirty minutes with numerous people coming and going and I barely noticed them. But when you came, I immediately felt God bring you to my attention. Isn't that incredible? God loves you so much He arranged for a complete stranger to tell you He knows about your circumstances and that He's got good plans for your future.' He looked astonished and perplexed all at once.

'Do you know about Jesus?' I asked.

In response to the confusion on his face I could see he did not so I began to tell him; that God loves us, that He sent His son Jesus to die for us, and that He wants to have real relationship with us as opposed to formulaic religious observance. For a quarter of an hour, we had an easy dialogue in that vein. But with time marching on, I said my goodbyes and left to catch my flight. God was not done however. As I walked away, I felt Him tell me to go back and offer to pray for my new German friend, Michael. We both knew I had ignored His prompt to do so a few minutes before! Now with my tail between my legs somewhat I went back, tapping Michael on his shoulder with 'It's me again.'

Perhaps our meeting was by now so unusual that me coming back offering to pray for him was not so strange. In any event, with a smile he readily agreed. I simply asked Jesus to guide him and show him how to get around the box to go forwards in life. When I finished, he looked at me, his eyes again brimming with tears as I urged him to reach out to Jesus who had reached out to him. Our parting moment was actually quite funny, a rather formal handshake slightly at odds with the very personal touch of heaven Michael had just experienced. Both smiling a little self-consciously, we said goodbye again, wishing each other the best for our respective lives.

But as I walked away seemingly calm, inside my joy was exploding! Not only was I moved by Michael's openness but even more by the astonishing love of God who had orchestrated our paths to cross in an airport of thousands. I marvelled at what Michael might be feeling, one moment weighed down by despair contemplating who knows what only to have a stranger tell him the next that God saw his plight, there was a way forward, and that Jesus loved him. The rest of the weekend was spent enjoying a top Scottish hotel with my colleagues and no end of luxury around me. But fun though it was, it did not come anywhere near matching my delight at having seen God reach out in kindness to someone so desperate. Just as Jesus described, God looks for the one lost sheep, even among thousands.

Over time, that example of God working in my life to touch others became a regular occurrence, although, if I am honest, I felt rather on my own as I did not know many other people doing the same. Thankfully there are many more today. But the encounters were always immensely precious, with God typically using me at a point of vulnerability or crisis in someone's life. Yes, each circumstance caught me unawares requiring fresh courage to initiate conversation, but the outcomes were invariably humbling as I saw God delight and shock people with His knowledge of them and love.

Towards the end of this decade, another significant change came my way as I joined a new community of believers in London. I kind of stumbled across their beginnings but was excited to have found like-minded Christians intent on pursuing the presence of God. In time we became King's Gate church[13]. More surprising to me, however, was to find myself involved in its leadership, signalling a new journey learning to serve, lead, and build with all the responsibility that entails. It became a big part of my life as I, with others, threw my heart into growing this new community. And whilst it was a season of steep growth and learning tough lessons of leadership, I loved this community.

We were certainly a distinctive tribe with a team at the helm and different people leading and serving in a way you generally do not see in the wider church; we sought to foster on purpose a culture of preferring one another. It was in that community I first found myself recognised as the prophet I had come to realise I was, refreshingly given freedom to operate in that function as prophet, preacher, and leader. The joy was being in a company of people who wanted to make space for one another to a degree I had not experienced before. It was also a place where lifelong friendships were formed. And as time has passed, I have learnt it is quite a rare thing to find oneself running after God as one with others also running as hard. I am genuinely humbled to say I found that at King's Gate.

Notes

[13] www.kingsgate.org.uk

12
JOY

I have drunken deep of joy,
And I will taste no other wine tonight.
Percy Bysshe Shelley

If the need to live deep in hope to overcome life's difficulties was the biggest lesson God had taught me thus far, I was about to learn He had another.

Joy made an entrance.

I don't mean the odd moment of laughter or humour but something inordinately deeper and vaster. It seemed to creep in on the heels of hope although I had not been looking for it in the same way. It was not that I didn't expect to experience joy as God's child but I did not see its connection to hope or appreciate its power.

But when it arrived, I realised its inevitability because it is impossible to know great hope and not great joy as well!

Hope, with all the lightness and optimism it brings, so obviously clears the way for joy to follow as the very characteristic that expresses delight in the hope received. First, I began to experience tangible joy in my times with God as I poured out my love on Him from a hope-filled heart. If I occasionally began with any heaviness, my familiarity with the road to hope would soon lead me there after which joy would promptly arrive.

Its effect was to produce a lightness in me which increasingly remained after these times with God, although the word doesn't fully convey joy's breadth. Joy is multi-dimensional, not only a gentle stream but a roaring waterfall too. Once hope cleared space for its entrance, it never really left me even if its level fluctuated at times in the swirl of life events. Joy was present and active in my life, not just in my times with God but at some level all the time. It caused my dialogue with God to transform, my inner world habitually more joyful as I praised God in everything; easily compelled by a joyful heart.

I discovered too that gratitude is the doorbell which invites it in. How so? The more a posture of gratitude is adopted the more there is joy as the mind and heart comprehend with gladness where gratitude is due. And as joy comes in increased measure, an expanding cycle begins of gratitude leading to joy leading to yet more gratitude and yet more joy. In fact, when joy is on the loose it has unstoppable momentum and impact! Over time it lit me up inside with its fire and delight, warming me and consequently the life I lived. I began to find that no amount of dull, day-to-day mundanity became somewhere I couldn't find joy because, like hope, its source was union with God on the inside and not external circumstance.

The lesson was clear. **Joy is a huge part of abundant life and the bedfellow of hope.**

Actually, when I began to look to the Bible to understand it more, I was surprised to see how 'serious' God is about it. For example, Jesus was the most joyful man who ever lived (Psalm 45:7) which was remarkable given His weighty assignment to save humanity, and the suffering that involved. The Kingdom of heaven itself consists of joy together with righteousness and peace[14] while the very presence of God is full of joy (Psalm 16:11). This means if we internally turn our hearts towards God we can access it.

I love that joy supplies us with strength (*the joy of the Lord is our strength*' (Nehemiah 8:10)). I was seeing that evidenced in my life as I embraced joy, becoming stronger and more vibrant than I had ever been. And if on occasion life's buffeting diminished my joy, I now knew how to go back to Jesus quickly to exchange my heaviness for it.

I was puzzled, however, that the Bible tells us Jesus endured the cross in anticipation of the joy ahead of Him (Hebrews 12:2). I could not conceive of any measure of joy that could be sufficient for Him to go through the horror of the cross. It was not just crucifixion He suffered, as dreadful as that is, but also the weight of the sin and sickness of all humanity.

Life-changing understanding about this mystery only came some years later through an encounter I had.

On a birthday of no particular importance, I went to my local park to spend time with God, drinking in the late autumn colours. As I walked and talked with Him, I began to experience really intense joy with a sense I can only describe as being in a very 'high' place in the heavenlies, close to God. At the same time, the German word 'Hochzeit' came to mind. Coincidentally I had been studying German at the time and had just learnt the word for wedding, 'Hochzeit', which consists of two words 'hoch' (high) and 'Zeit' (time). Although perplexed that it came to mind, I thought God was simply using a German word somewhat humorously to describe the sense of height I had during my walk.

But that forty-five minute experience of joy was beyond anything I had known before. It came out of nowhere but was so powerful and intense it eclipsed everything in my life prior. Yes, I mean EVERYTHING. I had experienced wonderful times with God before then but, in that encounter, the joy I stepped into wiped them out in terms of comparable experiences. I did not forget them but it was as if my life began again at that time, simply because nothing I had lived until then was a match for the joy of those moments. Not only that, but the worst moments of my past were subsumed by the joy. I realised then that joy, fierce and consuming as it is, is undefeated even by suffering. A lightbulb moment for me.

Darkness really is utterly powerless against joy.

However, it was some time before I understood what had happened. I missed the obvious – that I had an encounter with a measure of bridal union with Jesus, which was why the German word for wedding had come to mind. Let me explain.

God the Father sent His Son as a sacrifice so that those who choose to enter into relationship with Him can become his sons and daughters. But Jesus came as the bridegroom and His Father's reward to Him for His sacrifice will be receiving the Father's children who are prepared as His bride. Jesus made clear that all believers will have a place in heaven but only those who have intentionally pursued a life of intimacy with Him will be His bride, described in the parable of the wise and foolish virgins[1]. The final book of the Bible beautifully describes the culmination of these things at the end of time in a wedding feast[15], the ecstatic union into one of believers and Jesus reflected now in human marriage between bridegroom and bride.

Of course, the phenomenal degree of joy I experienced was but a taste of the joy to come in eternity. Honestly, there is no language to describe its potency; I wish it could be bottled for all. But after that experience, I understood Jesus endured the cross because of His desire for what is ahead. He will receive His prize of union with the bride, the point of purest joy that can be known.

It will continue for all eternity.

The experience impacted me deeply because I realised that not only was this bridal union love the most intimate I could know, but it was where deepest joy lived. And if God was telling me I needed to continually live in joy, then that meant continually living in bridal love. Yes, scripture tells us we are privileged to be God's servants and friends, but there is a maturing process in intimacy which invites us to become a bride. We barely have any idea what that degree of union truly is, but incredibly He invites us into it every day of our lives:

'But the one who joins himself to the Lord is mingled into one spirit with him.' (1 Corinthians 6:17 TPT)

---

[1] Matthew 25:1-13

From the moment we give our lives to Him we are joined to Him. The word 'join' here means being glued or cleaved to or making two into one. The promise is priceless – of our spirit being mingled into perfect union with His in the heavenly romance of relationship with Him. There can be no greater privilege in life.

First we need revelation of the one-ness we step into in order to understand the invitation; that the fullness of Christ and therefore God is within us, and accessible by our believing it is.

> *'Your crucifixion with Christ has severed the tie to this life, and now your true life is hidden away in God in Christ'* (Colossians 3:3 TPT)

The invitation is to live a life of abiding in Him, or bridal union, with the promise that He will abide in us[16]. Out of that abiding, we can bear fruit for Him by having access to everything Jesus has access to, because we are blessed with every spiritual blessing of Christ's. This means if I have a friend who needs healing, once I see that healing is in Christ in me, I can release it to them. Though we, the people of God, have too often fallen short of being this powerfully effective for God on the earth, nevertheless our access to these treasures is true. Or as John, Jesus' beloved apostle, so beautifully put it *'...as He is, so also are we in this world.'* (1 John 4:17).

I have lived many years not grasping this and only tasting a little of what was freely available to me. But now that I do, my heart is aimed at being the expression of Christ to the world, as I live from a rested place in my spirit of union with, and abiding in, Him. This is the place of deepest joy.

But what about fun, humour, and laughter, which are all expressions of joy? Yes, God is the author of them. In the very act of creation, we see the Trinity delighting in their work. But the appearance of these things in the world can also mask the void of real joy. The world pursues happiness which generally requires the absence of difficulty in life to be attainable. And when it cannot be found - at best having no difficulty is temporary - it reaches for alternative experiences to fill the gap because, instinctively, we crave the true joy we are intended to know.

But joy is entirely different to worldly happiness. It has substance in itself because it is found in the heart of God and can be present regardless of circumstances. As it contains strength, it works powerfully to sustain us through difficult times. Worldly happiness, dependant on circumstances and without true substance, does not carry strength. When diagnosed with MS I despaired because my 'happiness', dependent as it was on good health, was now removed.

But once I pursued joy in Jesus, like striking oil, I found it had a force which was stronger than MS or any other difficult circumstance I faced. That is not to say I don't feel the sorrow of painful circumstances or that it is wrong to want relief from them, but when they are present joy is not overcome by them and neither should we be. Our hearts may ache, but we can still know deep down joy in the person of God, or as Paul more robustly said 'Our hearts ache, but we always have joy.' (2 Corinthians 6:10 NLT). They are not mutually exclusive.

At times, the joy I feel is so potent I literally do not know what to do with myself. I am blazing on the inside! Perhaps this is what

Peter meant in saying *'and though you do not see Him now, but believe in Him, you greatly rejoice with joy inexpressible and full of glory,'* (1 Peter 1:8).

Being honest, I have been amazed, as in the case of hope, that it was largely the pressure of MS in my life that precipitated my pursuit of joy once it appeared. I did not need to have MS to find joy, but am nevertheless grateful my journey took me to it. And I am by no means finished. I expect to taste ever-increasing joy throughout my life, not only because its supply is unending, but because Jesus made the outrageous claim He wants me to live in the same joy He did:

'These things I have spoken to you so that My joy may be in you, and that your joy may be made full.' (John 15:11)

How is that done? By abiding in Him which He tells us to do moments before this verse. He also tells us that thanksgiving takes us through the gates of His presence (Psalm 100:4) where there is fullness of joy (Psalm 16:11). Make no mistake, He has made the route to joy very plain.

But I am not sure many Christians have comprehended that an invitation into such depths of joy is on offer or what its transformative effects might be. Yet, there cannot be an argument that the world is desperate for joy. We were designed by God to know it, but in its absence, we substitute all manner of pleasures and activities such as exercise, sex, alcohol, and social media for it to medicate our inner turmoil. In right use, many of these are good things, but they were never intended to be our joy.

Joy is not pale or insipid as I once thought but powerful and formidable. If we lived in its depths, who could imagine the ways in which the world might be impacted. When I asked God to help me, I did not expect hope and joy to be lead actors in His answer. But they were. They changed my world and will continue to as I keep mining for more of their limitless supply. I am left, not only thankful to God, but now asking what an army equipped with weapons of hope and joy could look like. What bondages of our time could be shattered? What measure of heaven, full of hope and joy, might be seen as a result on earth?

Of course, these are not the only characteristics of God I or anyone else needs in their life. By picking them out as I do, I am not trying to present an unbalanced picture about what we should partake of in God. We need His fullness. But I am describing the aspects of His nature which, more than others, led my rescue from difficulty blasting a hole through its darkness.

And even if the possibilities for an army of people equipped with God's hope and joy are a stretch in human imagining, they are certainly not with God. God says if we ask Him, He will tell us great and unsearchable things (Jeremiah 33:3 NIV). So I am asking. What kind of people is He searching for, for that army? What might an army kitted out in hope and joy look like? How might it then invade and takeover where darkness has controlled?

Will anyone wonder and dream with God in these terms?

Notes

[14] *"...for the kingdom of God is not eating and drinking, but righteousness and peace and joy in the Holy Spirit.:* Romans 14:17

[15] Revelation 19:7

[16] John 15:4 *'Abide in me, and I in you. As the branch cannot bear fruit by itself, unless it abides in the vine, neither can you, unless you abide in me.'* (ESV) *'So you must remain in life-union with me, for I remain in life-union with you. For as a branch severed from the vine will not bear fruit, so your life will be fruitless unless you live your life intimately joined to mine.'* (TPT)

13

BROKEN BONES

I don't think of all the misery,
but of the beauty that still remains.
Anne Frank

'Mum, don't worry! I am meeting someone in Charlotte so we can travel on together. I'll call you when I'm back in a week's time.' With that reassurance I rang off, keen to finish my packing.

I was really excited, about to begin a week's holiday. I was going to a Christian conference in the USA, situated remotely in the North Carolina hills. For only fifty delegates, it would be an intimate gathering with several renowned speakers and prophets due to teach. I had heard that the Moravian Falls location was special because of its thin spiritual atmosphere as a result of Moravian Christians praying there at length. It was the perfect place to encounter God therefore.

Early indications were that the week would not disappoint. Delegates were accommodated in charming wooden cabins dotted across the steep hills. I found myself sharing a cabin with Kathryn, an ex-police officer.

Quickly we settled into the conference routine of worship times and talks, walks in the wooded hills, new friendships, and general basking in the beautiful location. But there was particular excitement on Wednesday (day 3) as the late Bob Jones, a renowned prophet, was coming to speak. Kathryn was so excited she found us seats in the front row. We wanted to absorb everything we could from this wise man.

The evening he spoke was as rich in spiritual food as expected, although quiet in atmosphere as we listened attentively. To finish the evening Bob and his wife Bonnie were to pray for each of us but, mindful that he was an elderly man, the leaders told us it would be brief.

Against that backdrop, what happened to me next was unexpected to say the least. I am not naturally a dramatic person. But after Bonnie prayed for me, I felt myself being filled with Holy Spirit to a degree I had never experienced before. The sense of 'weight' or presence of the Spirit was so strong on me I had difficulty staying upright[17]. But even when I got back to my seat there was more to come.

To my great surprise, I began to feel incredible joy rising up within me causing me to bubble up with gales of laughter. Although in the past I had seen this happen to other people[18], if I am honest, I had been somewhat sceptical about the authenticity of their experience. But my doubts were swept away in that moment as the joy which filled me was so real and wonderful; I could not help but laugh and laugh and laugh! Actually, it was slightly embarrassing because I was noisy in an otherwise quiet room.

As one of the leaders began to close the meeting, I heard him say, 'Holy Spirit is so obviously on this girl that, if I were you, I would ask her for prayer once we end the meeting.' He looked enquiringly at me, 'Is that ok?'

'Of course,' I answered, struggling to get the words out through my laughter.

With that I stood up and turned around to see a queue of people forming quickly. I was more than happy to share whatever I was receiving so reached out my hand to touch the first person, praying a release of Holy Spirit on her. Immediately, the power of the Spirit swept through me in such strength that I fell backwards onto the floor still laughing. It was not an awkward fall so I simply got up to pray for the next person. I reached out my hand to touch her, repeating the prayer. The same thing happened; I fell backwards.

However, this time was different. I felt a surge of pain in my right leg. I drew my breath trying to figure what was going on. At first, no one noticed anything was wrong except Kathryn who signalled as much to the leader. Speaking to the whole group, he asked them to begin to pray in the Spirit[19], no doubt wondering how anything could be wrong given the heavenly atmosphere of worship and prayer we were in.

Once it became clear I could not get up, and after a bit of conversation with leaders about whether someone should carry me back to my cabin, instinct told me I needed to be taken to hospital. Although I did not think anything was seriously wrong, I suspected my painful leg was the result of more than a sprained ankle needing some medical attention given the absence of a healing miracle following the group's prayers. (More on that later.)

Fast forward a couple of hours and a doctor at the nearest hospital came to report on the results of x-rays.

After his opening words of, 'You have shattered your leg', an unhelpful joke I thought in the circumstances, I waited for him to continue telling me, perhaps, that I had torn a ligament or tendon. But he did not and with astonishment I realised he was completely serious.

'Because we are a regional hospital, we can't deal with this kind of injury so we are sending you to a central hospital in Winston-Salem.' he explained. 'Winston where?' I thought to myself.

He continued, 'You're going to need surgery.' I was stunned. This could not be happening. Just a few hours before I was reflecting on what an amazing week it was turning out to be. Now I was in a hospital in America being told I had a serious injury. Before I knew it, I was in an ambulance on my way, incredulous that this had happened but hugely grateful to Kathryn, my only friend of sorts at that moment in the US, who promised to follow me in her truck.

It felt somewhat surreal. I tried to call my brother in the UK from the ambulance to tell him what had happened but could not get through. In the meantime, I chatted to the ambulance man who told me that the hospital we were going to was a major trauma centre so I would be in good hands. Remarkably, I was not in horrendous pain which I later discovered surprised everyone. I gave my pain a four out of ten rating when asked by medics, but they later told me they would have expected it to be a twelve given my injuries. Perhaps a bit of shock plus Holy Spirit relief kicked in?

When we got to the second hospital, it was about midnight. I only vaguely remember hours of scans and x-rays ensuing with me falling in and out of sleep throughout, although repeatedly telling medics I had MS when I woke up in case it was important they knew. I had no idea whether it was.

When morning came, I found myself settled in a room woken by the greeting of an orthopaedic surgeon. A jovial man in his fifties, he began rather cheerfully, 'The bad news is you have about 12 or 13 fractures in your tibia (lower right leg).' I gulped at this news. Not surprisingly, his cheerfulness grated somewhat with the information delivered.

He continued, 'We would usually see this in someone who has been in a very bad car crash or jumped out of a two-storey building. Do you want to tell me what happened?'

In the previous hours, I had described the events to doctors several times in my waking moments, but I gathered there was some disbelief about my story.

I began again, 'I'm on holiday from the UK in Moravian Falls at a conference. Yesterday evening as the conference group was together, I fell backwards onto carpeted floor and this happened.' I pointed to my leg having decided there was no point confusing him with talk about God. After a pause I went on, sensing his puzzlement, 'I didn't fall from any height and no alcohol was involved.' I wondered if he was checking the credibility of my story; had I had been drinking or taking drugs. In any event, he seemed to believe me at that point.

'It must have been one of those freak falls then.' He offered sympathetically. 'It can happen if you fall at an angle, like the wood of a wooden door splitting the whole way down. You have been most unfortunate.' What he was referring to was the fact that, due to the fractures, the bone in my lower leg was effectively 'folded up' like a closed accordion (horrible, makes me feel queasy even writing that.) In a sense, it was extraordinary I had not realised the seriousness sooner given the state of my leg. But I had been so absorbed in God's touch and then making the decision to go to hospital, that the notion of anything being seriously wrong when I was still composed and able to talk to people just hadn't crossed my mind. And as a 'by the way', he also told me MS had not made me more prone to fractures. My bone density had been checked and was normal.

The outcome of our conversation, however, was confirmation of the earlier bombshell; I needed to have surgery on my leg before flying back to the UK. It was scheduled for the following day unless things deteriorated i.e. I could not keep wiggling my toes which, needless to say, I kept doing rather obsessively for the rest of the day. And 'no, it could not wait until family arrived' he told me firmly, meaning I needed to accept the reality of impending major surgery without them with me (gulp…).

I like to think I handle crises well or maybe I mistake that for the grace of God. Either way, although I was on my own on the other side of the world with a seriously messed up leg, (the 'bad' MS leg no less), no family or friends with me, not even sure where I was in the US, and now entirely in the hands of doctors I didn't know, I felt really peaceful with an assurance I was safe in God's care.

Of course, the events raised huge God questions. When Holy Spirit is moving it is only ever for good, so how could this have happened? It made no sense and, even more so, given the heavenly atmosphere in which it occurred. But I knew I needed to put my questions aside to focus mentally and emotionally on getting through the ordeal. And to my surprise, I was able to hold onto God and the joy from the previous evening which, remarkably, I still felt wrapped in. Actually that was a very good thing as I needed to pass on as much peace and calm as I could to my distressed family once they heard the news.

A day later I came round to the booming voice of the anaesthetist in the recovery room saying, 'Honey, you sure gave us some hardware challenges in there but we figured it out – it's all good.' What he meant, I later found out, was that the original plan of inserting one piece of metal in my leg had not worked so three pieces had to be made instead for different places. That, at least, explained why the estimated two-hour surgery had become nine and a half hours, but beyond that I didn't care – I was just pleased to see my leg now apparently straight again in a cast! And I was told the surgery had been successful.

Thus began a five day stay in hospital which turned out to be quite extraordinary. By now Kathryn had arrived and was waiting to greet me as I was wheeled back to my room. I was so glad to see a familiar face. Although really a relative stranger to me after only three days' acquaintance, recognising I was kind of on my own in the US that week, she generously took the place of friend, sister, and more at the time. She even selflessly gave up attending the remainder of the conference to stay with me. I am forever in her debt for the kindness she showed. Definitely an example of love with feet on it.

By my reckoning, the first unusual feature of the hospital stay was that I felt so well after surgery, fresh as a daisy in fact. I was not remotely tired or anxious; incredibly, just joyful! Kathryn and I chatted at length about the whole saga until at one point, somewhat tentatively, she asked if I remembered what my leg and knee looked like after the initial impact. Actually, I remembered very clearly because, as I looked down in those first moments, I could not believe what I was seeing. My right knee was somewhere else… No, I had not lost my mind and yes, it was still attached to my body. But it was now somehow positioned in a different direction – horrifying to see.

People often say that in moments of crisis time seems to slow and so it did for me. In what felt like slow motion, I looked down, saw my knee with incredulity, barely took in what had happened to my leg, and turned my head away. Then, in what felt like a good five minutes later although it was probably less than one, the leader, as I have said, asked the group to pray for me. As they did, I kept my gaze elsewhere, trying to compute what I had seen and keep calm. They only prayed for a few minutes but once they stopped, I turned my head back to look at my leg. And when I did, I could scarcely believe what I saw. Without having 'felt' anything move, my right knee was now back in the correct position on my leg, with the rest of the lower leg still folded up as described.

Astonishing – what had just happened?? But in the drama of the situation, the urgent overtook the extraordinary. I was brought into conversation about what to do and how to get me from the remote cabin to hospital. In the whirl of activity that followed, I had not remarked on it. I did not know if anyone else had seen what I had.

But Kathryn, it transpired, had seen the very same as me. In the day before surgery neither of us said anything. I was focussed on contacting people and preparing myself for it. But post-surgery, she wanted to know if I was aware of what happened and grasped that an extraordinary miracle had occurred in those minutes.
I certainly had and was delighted now to have a witness with whom to voice my amazement. While I was in no doubt about what I had seen, it was encouraging and validating to hear Kathryn describe it as well, particularly as she was accustomed to paying attention to the detail of accident scenes as a police officer.

The obvious question it begs, of course, is why God worked a miracle with my knee and not the whole leg. That is another 'I don't know' moment in my life. But what I do know, and appreciated many times in the following years, was how hugely disabled I probably immediately would have become had my knee remained as messed up as it initially was. Bad though the other fractures were, and there's more to tell, the fact that my knee did not require surgery meant I have been able to walk since recovering from the accident, albeit with effects of the surgery and MS. Had the miracle not occurred, my future would almost certainly have been very different.

However, I was yet to find out that God had more surprising things in store for that hospital stay!

The first 'divine' set up was when two hospital chaplains came to see me. They were young men, Paul and Mark. Because they were Christians, I told them openly and enthusiastically about the conference, how wonderfully I had experienced Holy Spirit, and that a key theme of the week was hearing God through prophetic gifts. However, once I saw their stony-faced reactions, I realised they did not believe the gifts of the Spirit such as prophecy and healing exist today. Some Christians don't, a view called cessationism[20]. It was quite amusing because Kathryn either ignored their reactions or did not notice them and proceeded to tell them what God was saying about their lives.

Despite their initial discomfort, within minutes it became clear that what Kathryn was saying was both accurate and hugely impacting as we saw them visibly moved. But to my great surprise, I began to hear God speaking to me about them too.

After a bit of internal argument between me and God along the lines of 'Surely not God – I'm the patient with a broken leg,' and His reply, 'Actually yes, tell them what I've told you', I asked them if I could add to what Kathryn had said. It was almost funny to see the conflict on their faces; on the one hand their hesitation as chaplains on the basis that I, the patient, should not be ministering to them but, on the other, their human desire to hear from God despite my patient status.

Desire won the day and they told me to go ahead! When I did, the room became wonderfully filled with the presence of God as I prophesied telling them exciting plans God had for their lives and how He would transform areas of struggle for them into areas of strength. When we finished, their demeanour had completely changed, their faces lit up with delight at what they heard and the experience of God's touch. They stayed chatting, clearly now at ease, a sense of trust in us replacing their earlier caution, and in no hurry to leave. Final proof that we had blown a hole through their theology that God did not speak through prophecy today was when Paul's pager went off and he told Mark to ignore it!

But that was just the beginning. Over the following days, time after time God would open up conversations between staff and me about Jesus, giving me pictures, words of knowledge[21] or prophecies for them. One night when I wanted to sleep, I was somewhat irritated by a nurse who kept coming into my room for no apparent reason, until I figured out she must want me to pray for her too. Apparently, word had gone round I had done so for others.

Noticeably, staff goodwill towards me kept growing that week. One nurse came in to see me on her day off to continue our conversation about Jesus, and another even brought me a gift before I left to thank me for my prayers for her. I was honestly just being myself, but somehow God kept sneaking into every conversation without any intentionality on my part.

It showed me that simply being loving, warm, and kind releases the goodness of heaven. This attracts people because it isn't their usual experience of life. The more I loved on people, (just being kind), the more God showed up for them, (releasing words), the more touched they were, and the more my delight in Him increased. Far from draining me, I seemed to have more, not less, to give out - that perpetual circle of love in God again.

Truthfully, in spite of the traumatic events that put me there, my memory of that hospital stay is that it was full of God making His presence felt in beautiful ways and, rather bizarrely, a good measure of joy. I was in awe that in my weakness, stuck in a hospital bed, barely able to do anything for myself, I was being used by God's strength. The paradox of a hard time being marked by the beauty of God's fingerprints again. It was the ''upside down-ness' of the Kingdom of God…

A week after the accident I was back in the UK having been rescued by my brother - awful timing for him and his wife who had just had their fourth child but someone had to accompany me home. Once back, I found myself in a London hospital seeing a new orthopaedic surgeon. After further x-rays, however, I was in for a shock. Apparently, my right leg was not straight, my right foot was at an outwards angle of more than 5%. I was stunned. Not only had no one explained that in the US but the UK surgeon told me that that level of deviation would not be accepted in the UK as expectation around surgical outcomes had advanced. But because I had just had a big operation, he did not advise another given the increased risks of bone not healing and infection. All of which meant he told me the best course for me was to live with this far from ideal outcome.

Leaving aside my slightly dented vanity over the now obvious disfigurement of my right leg, the long-term implications of the surgery were more concerning. Because my right foot was misaligned, over time I would be putting unnatural strain on my ankle, knee, and back which the surgeon predicted would almost inevitably lead to complications. Down the track, he talked about me possibly needing more surgery with back pain likely to develop. Not news I wanted to hear or, indeed, accepted as inevitable, knowing that God's power and desire to heal supersedes natural facts true though they may be. But for now, according to the surgeon, there was nothing to be done except to get on with a six-month recovery. Which is what I did. And by the end, I was very grateful to find that the accident had had no effect on the MS. This meant, when I did get rid of crutches, I walked the same way I had before, albeit with a newly positioned foot.

Positives aside, however, I did realise breaking my leg was both traumatic and beyond unfortunate; I absolutely didn't need more physical problems. But, conversely, the most striking and gratifying outcome of the whole episode to me was to reveal my progress on the inward transformation journey I had set out on some years before.

On the question of healing, I am glad to say my professed belief in Jesus as Healer stood the test of me now having additional physical problems to deal with. I chose not to see the accident as a 'double whammy' of sorts on my health as some friends did. Yes, the event was traumatic and had potentially significant implications for my body going forwards but, in my new place of thinking, I had a different revelation of the future with Jesus as Healer. That meant I did not need to even ask whether healing of the newest problems would be a question for God. If His nature was always to heal and bring heaven to earth where there are no injuries, then it followed that could be my confident expectation.

God was not challenged by the effects of my surgery. As well as metal dissolving in bodies (yes, I meant to write that!), I had heard of many medically verified miracles of bones being readjusted and healed - hadn't I seen that with my knee? And from my first meeting with the UK surgeon, I had decided not to absorb his gloomy predictions of what lay ahead. I did not know precisely how God would work but, knowing His nature and desire for healing, I determined to expect the best.

On the question of inward transformation, I also found I had reason to be encouraged. When any of us sets out to be changed, it can be difficult to know what progress we are making. Often it takes adversity to show us when pressure exposes the truth of the heart.

Certainly, this accident ticked the pressure box. But I am glad to say I do not remember lasting moments of feeling sorry for myself, being angry with God or despairing about the future. Instead, there were signs of the embedding of new habits – plenty of gratitude, me more often looking for the good and not the bad, and a steady confidence that God was for me.

Looking back, I am so grateful for this heart growth because by any measure the accident was an unwelcome curveball. However, one tries to reason why or how it happened, it was not from God. Only the Devil brings destruction. But newly equipped as I then was to deal with it, I saw that what the enemy sent to derail me had abysmally failed.

In fact, I became stronger in God through it. In the recovery months off work, I spent hours with Him connecting more deeply. And in moments when MS plus a broken leg felt like too much, God would remind me that *'our momentary, light affliction is producing for us an eternal weight of glory far beyond all comparison...'*.[22]

That came as a powerful perspective shift to remind me that living well through this challenge would achieve heavenly glory for me. A weighty promise.

When I had fully recovered, I was gratified to see that the paths of hope and joy, as well as other qualities I hoped God was ploughing in my heart, were at least well-trodden. Far from being reduced, they expanded and deepened as I returned to work with greater levels of them than I'd had before. The beginnings of living by faith and believing the Healer, instead of by sight with beliefs capped by medical reports, were more deeply rooted in me.

That meant that broken bones or not, my view of the future with God was richer than ever in possibility.

And that was its own miracle.

Notes

[17] An example of this in the Bible is when King Solomon was dedicating the temple he built. The priests couldn't stand to minister to God because of the weight of the glory of God present (2 Chronicles 5:13-14).

[18] A 'manifestation of the Spirit' is when there is an obvious physical effect of the Holy Spirit on a person. This was famously seen on Pentecost when people in Jerusalem thought the believers were drunk after they received Holy Spirit, evidently by their behaviour i.e. joyful, unsteady on their feet, loud! The Bible and history shows us there can be varied manifestations such as laughter (God's joy), shaking (the reason the 'Quakers' were so named), people immobile or seemingly asleep with the weight of God on them (revival meetings of Mariah Woodworth-Etter).

[19] Praying 'in the Spirit' or in tongues is praying in a supernatural language of Holy Spirit, one of the gifts available to believers (1 Corinthians 12). The Bible tells us the person praying in tongues builds themselves up as they pray mysteries to God (1 Corinthians 14:2-4).

[20] Cessationism is an evangelical theological system which believes, among other things, that supernatural healing and use of the gifts of Holy Spirit, such as tongues and prophecy, are not intended by God for today's church but ended once the last of the apostles Jesus appointed had died.

[21] A word of knowledge is a gift of Holy Spirit which provides a person with insight or knowledge they couldn't otherwise have had so that God can use them in some way (1 Corinthians 12:8). For example, a believer might see/hear within them 'left arm' as a prompt that someone present needs prayer for healing in the left arm. Jesus used the word of knowledge when he met the Samaritan woman telling her she had several husbands. The accuracy of His insight opened her heart to hearing more.

[22] 2 Corinthians 4:17

14

INTIMACY

What wonder is it if I be set on fire by Thy presence and be utterly consumed, when Thou art a fire always burning and never failing…

Thomas à Kempis

While I have described my God-wards journey with hope and joy, I would not be an honest storyteller if I did not talk about the deeper context. That is that the treasures of everything I discovered in God came out of a life of being close to Him.

Intimacy.

I realise talk of intimacy may be unfamiliar, even uncomfortable, for some. Can we really be that close to the Creator of the universe? While it is an astonishing thought, perhaps it is less so when we remember love motivated His dying for us. And love invites relationship; friendship but also that of lover. And inevitably that stirs a like response in us. Yes, we can actually know Jesus as the bridegroom who is coming back for His bride.

When I began to pursue knowing Him, I did not see it in those terms. I was just trying to find out if there really was a depth and reality to knowing God which would speak to my devastated heart. That began as far back as my Friday nights all those years before. But it did not take long before the beginnings of friendship with Him turned into the passion of the Beloved, me, for Him, the Bridegroom. Then I could relate to King Solomon's words as my heart responded to His, *'I am my beloved's and my beloved is mine,'* (Song of Songs 6:3). Although in ensuing years I did not feel I had arrived at a place of intimacy with Him as I struggled with the overwhelm of MS, an acute awareness of my need for Him grew.

Often, I felt like David when he said, *'As the deer longs for streams of water, so I long for you, O God.'* (Psalm 42:1 NLT). I knew I needed to drink from life from Him every day. As a result, I increasingly carved out daily time alone with Him to give Him my undivided attention.

But it was not until I fully gave up resentment at God about my health and other demands that I was able to experience a deeper connection. While I hung onto them, they were a barrier to closeness. When I eventually did, I realised fullness of life is only to be had in relationship with Jesus because He is the essence of life (*'In him was life; and the life was the light of men.'* (John 1:4 BSB)).

Being healed or married would be wonderful expressions of His life in mine, but if I saw them as life's peak, I would be disappointed. I had been burned in the past by the mistake of misplaced hope in promises above Jesus Himself. But when I understood my error, I grasped that He is the doorway to true life which is union with God and His love. That is the only truly solid and life-giving place of being all humanity aches for.

We are surprised by this only if we do not understand our level of connectedness to Him. What I mean is that we were created through Him and are held together by Him (Colossians 1:16-17). Remarkably the Bible tells us that if for a second He stopped holding us together, we would disintegrate[23]. I always feel a sadness for Him when I read '*He came to His own, and His own people did not receive Him*' (John 1:11 ESV). Imagine a designer who designs an adventure park, where thousands go for enjoyment, but they deny that the designer had any part in it and refuse him entry. That is what we do when we don't invite Jesus into our lives. He only wants willing lovers, so He allows us that freedom.

In time, God pointed me to the story of Hannah in the Bible to expand my understanding of true oneness with God. As we are introduced to Hannah in 1 Samuel 1, we read of a young married woman going to the temple each year to pray that God would grant her a child. Rather curiously, we read that God prevented her becoming pregnant. As time passes, Hannah's journey becomes more painful as year after year she fails to conceive. But finally, we read of a changed conversation between Hannah and God in the temple. In it she tells God that if He will give her a son, she will give him back in service to Him.

What changed? Something huge, but we can miss it if we do not read carefully. In this new prayer for a son, Hannah shows a level of yielded-ness to God she had not before. Previously, she had been asking for a son for her life and fulfilment; there was no talk of him being part of her worship back to God. But the pain of her journey over time changed her heart, not in bitterness against

God at not getting what she wanted, but **in love towards God** so that she offered her whole life to Him. And when she got to that wholly surrendered place, her request for a son became an abandoned offering of him in worship to God.

A massive change. For the first time, she truly gave God her whole heart and life.

The beauty of the story is that He not only gave her a son, Samuel, the prophet over Israel no less, but five other children as well. The point is that even when we think we are sacrificing we are not; the sacrifice is all on God's part who gave His Son in place of our punishment. God had much more to give Hannah than she asked, but it took a painful journey towards full surrender for her to yield her will to Him.

That yielding was what God taught me.

In my 'Thinking Bootcamp' phase, a large part of my seeking God was to relieve my horrible despair. He loves us so much that for a time He will not take issue with that kind of bargain – give to me God and I will give a bit to you. But He wants to bring true freedom to our hearts, which is a pursuit of Him for His sake and not as a means to an end. Once we arrive at that honest love, we find that the things we need and desire flow towards us. That is how it was for me. It took me many years to get there but, once I finally understood I needed to pursue Him without agenda, I let all my demands go.

Let me tell you that there is a glorious liberty in coming to God with that heart. There is nothing like it – no subtext - just a pure desire to love Him and be loved back. And increasingly as I experienced this new yielded-ness to God, I would prefer to be alone with Him rather than socialising with friends, as my joy in those intimate moments knew no limits (and my friends are *wonderful*).

Now people often ask me how I pursue Him. I have no formula. My answer is in different ways according to His leading. He constantly changes the moves in this dance of love, just as in a good relationship, no two conversations are the same. I love spending time worshipping and loving Him alongside worship music, although when the music is distracting, I still hear Him loud in silence. I also **love** reading His Word, ever-amazed at the ways it comes alive as I ask Holy Spirit to illumine it. It really is *the* best book – in fact, a library of books all revealing God.

And prayer is an exciting adventure as He meets with me. From experiencing internal visions with understanding of His message; to moments when my joy is so strong I am compelled to move around, loudly expressing my delight; to yet other moments when I see Him in heaven's throne room with the weight of His glory tangible to me like thick honey.

Inevitably, out of that intimacy there is a journey towards hearing His voice more clearly. It continues to come in a myriad of new ways. I began to understand what Jesus meant when He said that man does not live by the material only, (i.e. bread alone), but by every word that comes from the mouth of God. That is because God's voice contains His essence. He is the Word, feeding our spirits and souls. There is *nothing* like it, materially or otherwise. His voice leads us into knowing we are perfectly loved and safe because we are in a living relationship with the One who holds everything together and in whom there is eternal life. This is the place of deepest peace there is.

Farther down this road of intimacy, I began to realise if I wanted to walk in a deeper relationship with God, I had to prioritise closeness with Him over everything else. I would often ponder that Jesus told His followers they would do greater works than He did; a staggering promise and one I want to be part of even if it is not yet fulfilled generally among His followers. And even though I had established a habit of spending time with God, I was aware of the constant need to fight for it in a world of much distraction. Now, I try to keep Him in front of my eyes all the time; to walk in more of Him, not only in my set apart times with Him but continually. He is my most ferocious pursuit, not for my own promotion, but to be a conduit for His life on earth. A work in progress of course.

My belief is that there is no ceiling on encounter with God from His side. A standard-bearer for me is Enoch who walked with God, so pleasing to Him that he did not die but was taken up to heaven (Genesis 5:24; Hebrews 11:5). Although Enoch did not have available to him under the old covenant the oneness in Christ that we do with the Holy Spirit living in us, he still lived in astonishing and rare communion with God.

But where are those who are reaching for this deeper oneness under the new covenant? And what will that look like for those whose hunger takes them there? The Bible surely tells us when it says, *'I have betrothed you to one husband, that I may present you as a chaste virgin to Christ.'* (2 Corinthians 11:2 NKJV).

Yes, our betrothal to Jesus offers us that degree of union! It is only waiting to be found by those who seek Him so earnestly that they might fully represent Him on earth.

I am not ashamed to say that this is now my primary life pursuit. There is nothing better to live towards – to be part of His bride and, from that place of oneness, to discover and live out the heart and dreams of God to the end that He would say, 'Well done, good and faithful servant'.

Notes

[23] Colossians 1:17 *He is before all things, and in Him all things hold together.*

15

DERAILMENT

Still round the corner there may wait,
a new road or a secret gate.
J.R.R. Tolkien

'See you soon Sarah, we're going to have a great week!' I enthused at the end of our call, excited at the prospect of a visit to one of my closest friends in Glasgow. Sarah and I had been violinists in the same year at music college, bonding through our love of classical music and shared faith. Although our paths had since diverged somewhat, she now a wife and Mum, we had remained extremely close.

I arrived at Gatwick Airport the following day for my flight to Glasgow. Typically, at airports I needed wheelchair assistance for the final stage of getting to departure gates, but, as I could still walk through security myself and pass time in a café, I relished doing so, savouring the sense of independence as I embarked on rare travels.

But something was not right on this occasion. Internally, I found myself asking God with an edge to my inner voice what was up with my walking. The edge was my alarm – this kind of difficulty walking was not normal for me. Almost immediately, the gospel story of Lazarus who was raised from the dead came to mind. Although I knew it was God prompting me to read it, I churlishly told Him I had read it before. Sometimes we, or maybe that should be I, really do say stupid things to God; of course, He knew I had read it. I waited for a response. Perhaps not unsurprisingly, there wasn't any.

Ten minutes later, with an increasing sense of panic, I repeated my question to God. This time when the Lazarus story came to mind, I quickly pulled a Bible from my bag and turned to it chastened by fear (John 11:1-44). If you are not familiar with the story, it goes something like this. Jesus was a close friend of Lazarus and his sisters, Mary and Martha. Although He was told Lazarus was very ill, it was a further two days before He set out for his home only to find that Lazarus had died and the funeral was over when He got there. The incredible turnaround in the narrative is that Jesus raised Lazarus to life from his tomb, His greatest miracle to that point.

Although there are many profound and awe-inspiring lessons that can be drawn from the events, not least that Jesus' actions prophesy His own resurrection, this time something new jumped off the page at me.

In large capitals in my heart, I noticed that things got worse for Lazarus before they got better because Jesus delayed going to visit to heal him, seemingly deliberately. Of course, the ultimate outcome is wonderfully redemptive with an even greater miracle than healing taking place precisely because of the delay. But with a sinking heart I wondered, 'Could God be hinting to me that things might get worse before they get better?' I was horrified and put it in the 'I must have heard wrong' box, trying to quash my unease.

That was around Easter time. But in July of that year things suddenly and fairly dramatically changed. I had a significant MS relapse, only the second since being diagnosed. In the space of a few days and 'out of the blue', my balance and ability to walk deteriorated a lot. Anyone who has experienced this will know how scary it is to tell your body to do things or move in a certain way, only to find that it does not and cannot. I could still walk but now much shorter distances and only very unsteadily, catching on to anyone or anything near me to help me balance. Having had many years of stable MS without relapses or 'attacks' as they are known, I was stunned, gripped by fear, just like the early years. Was this the beginning of a slippery downwards slope?

Medics immediately prescribed several days of intravenous steroids to try to reduce inflammation in the nerves. Being honest, I was much more shocked by this MS relapse than I had been by the broken leg four years before. To avoid having to chat to other people, I deliberately chose early morning appointments for my daily hospital visits. To my dismay, however, each day I found myself sitting beside MS patients having similar treatment. I suppose I should have suspected God might be setting me up to show His strength in my weakness as He had in America. But I didn't, absorbed as I was in my newly cratered world. Emotionally I was in bits.

In that place, however, I was to learn it really is about His strength and not mine. In spite of myself, each day I somehow found myself praying for someone such as the despairing young mother who had lost her sight to MS, or the nurse desperate to have a baby but who could not conceive. It was as if God's love would push me to disregard my self-focus, compelling me to offer prayer when seeing people's pain and need. And just as in the USA, the fact that God used me to show up in other people's lives in the middle of my own challenges both moved and encouraged me. If He was reaching out to others in my path, then I knew I was also high on His agenda. It was reassuring.

Unfortunately, in my case the steroids did not work so, once treatment was complete, I had to wait for the attack to pass which it did over time. But once that happened, I was confronted with a new reality – my walking and balance were now very significantly worse. (After an MS attack, sufferers generally do not fully regain their previous level of function although the extent to which they do will vary).

My gait was now undeniably 'odd' as my right knee did not bend when walking which meant I had to swing my right leg out to take a step – awkward, cumbersome, inelegant. For the first time, it was abundantly clear to the world at large that I had a significant disability. And it was during that time I remembered the moment at Gatwick, the sense I had that things might get worse before they got better. On reflection, it seemed I had heard God right.

I was shaken. Actually, worse than that. It felt like a grenade had gone off. A dramatic reaction? Perhaps not when you understand the big picture. At this point, I had been diagnosed for about fourteen years and been in a place of relative physical and emotional stability for some time. I did not expect it to change. Naïve of me? There were reasons for my thinking.

One was that before the relapse, I was actually doing quite well. Amazingly, I had hardly deteriorated physically in the fourteen years since MS diagnosis. After the first six months, things stopped getting worse; in fact, since that partial healing at the conference in my first year. Yes, I could not walk more than 300m once a day (a huge effort), could only walk slowly, had balance difficulties, and experienced other unpleasant symptoms (aka fierce muscle spasm, numbness, and electric currents). But my upper body was completely unaffected and, atypically, I had no change in energy levels. All of which meant that intense work pressures did not adversely affect me. So, while it would be wrong to say I was comfortable with the symptoms, I did become familiar with them and lived in a measure of calm once I realised every fluctuation did not mean I was about to have a massive relapse.

On top of that was the surprising degree of reassurance I received from medics. MS is notoriously unpredictable so most neurologists are reluctant to forecast its progress. But on several occasions a neurologist told me I was continually surprising them with my stability, one even saying he thought I would remain like this well into old age based on my seeming resilience and stable record.

MS, therefore, seemed to be securely ring-fenced in my life. I felt well, I was not getting worse, and my gladness in God was good. After all this time I was confident I would not get worse. The only change I expected was improvement - the healing God had promised.

But those presumptions had just fallen apart in my pseudo-stable world. I had very significantly deteriorated, the disease let out of its cage. No one could say I would not continue to go downhill. And that terrified me as I considered again whether it might do its worst leading to scenarios I have described - paralysis, incontinence, complete dependency on carers... Which all threw up fresh questions and challenges.

There was a new health reality. Until that point the fact that I had MS was not always immediately evident to people who met me. After the relapse, that changed overnight. My odd and unstable walk forced me to use a walking stick again, a big adjustment for me. Movement also tired me in a way it had not before. Everything became more difficult - I was slower, my movements careful and calculated because of instability, the obvious caution of someone continually trying not to fall. In my own home, I avoided going upstairs during the day unless I really needed to. Also, using a stick again made me feel like an old woman overnight, those low self-esteem issues back with a vengeance. And I increasingly seemed to have to be near a toilet; too much information I know but bladder weakness is common with MS.

Then there was the different way people generally now interacted with me. It wasn't bad or unkind but, for the first time, I could see in their eyes and their relating that I was in a new category in their minds. I was someone different, weak, outside 'normal' – not the same, in any event, as pre-relapse. And it kind of hurt. In my head, of course, I was still the same Jennifer -

capable, successful professionally, despite everything expecting better in the future - but now placed in a different space by society.

Added to this was the re-entry of fear about my new state. It was hard not to let it grip me. But stripped of my previous confidence that no further decline would occur, I had no idea how to navigate this uncertainty.

I realised then the early journey was like being in an 'MS' swimming pool. I was scared of the water and its depth as I could not swim; it was always neck level at least with times I was not sure I could feel the bottom. However, once I realised it was not so deep I would drown, I adjusted and learnt to swim i.e. function with MS. My fear reduced a little.

But this new situation had put me out into wild, open seas. There was no telling what conditions I would face, calm or stormy, and the ocean was bottomless. I was truly out of my depth. My fear and panic levels rocketed as well as the consuming loneliness and horror of being on my own with progression if it came. Even though I knew this kind of thinking was destructive, I struggled to resist it. Over and over, I would obsess about whether I was getting worse and how I would manage if I did.

The second challenge was a very practical one. Nine months previously I had finished my legal job and taken some time off before the next career move. Before the relapse, I had been in touch with head-hunters who were enthusiastic about placing me in a senior position in London. I had begun to do interviews. But in the middle of that process the relapse occurred. Once I recovered as much as I was going to, I remember getting in touch with them again only to be met by a completely different reaction. Suddenly they did not have any positions which were suitable. To my shock, I realised my working life future wasn't the same - the world now viewed me differently. Obvious questions began to bombard my mind. What employer would take the risk of hiring me now that compromised health was glaringly obvious? Was I finally hitting that wall of unemployability many with MS face although I needed to work, not least for an income? And if I did not get a job, what would I do?

But undoubtedly the greatest challenge of this season was the test of trust in God I faced. Before the relapse, I had found a way to live in a degree of wellness within the constraints of MS, mentally and physically. But now, with MS seemingly on the loose in my body and the possibility of not being able to work looming, the big question was whether the lessons I believed I had learned of trusting God were real. Was my level of trust only as deep as the severity of my historic symptoms, bad enough to me but by no means as severe as they might have been? Or was my trust really in my belief I would not get worse rather than God Himself? Regardless of what lay ahead, would I still walk in joy and hope shunning despair and bitterness?

Truthfully, I only found the answer after many weeks of wrestling with God. But when put to the test, I found I had at least moved beyond the tantrum toddler stage of years before when I flailed about with anger at God. This time as I reconsidered the Lazarus story prompt, I realised God had spoken to me to prepare me for what was coming as well as to point beyond it in hope. Not only would restoration come but, when it did, somehow there would be a greater outcome for me because of the added MS deterioration just as there had been for Lazarus who went from needing healing to resurrection from death. In fact, in my better moments, I saw that the comparison hinted at something rather glorious being ahead.

So, despite my fears, I realised the only way forward was to lean on God for help. Yes, there was an unwelcome familiarity about this place with my inside voice saying, 'This wasn't my plan, I'm scared.' The difference this time was that I had history in journeying with God that had shown me I could rely on Him, not even, but especially in the most desperate moments.

At this new juncture then, I reached my hand out to God to grasp His. I told Him I would trust in His faithfulness for my future, not only to survive, but in full expectation I would see His best in my life.

And although my situation was far scarier than in the past, to my surprise, somehow, I knew I now had a firmer grip on His hand.

16

DEEPER MINING

I have been bent and broken, but -
I hope - into a better shape.
Charles Dickens

As I climbed the stairs to the first floor, it felt somewhat like stepping back in time. I was in a charming old building in Gray's Inn, a cobble-stoned enclave in the heart of law in London. I had come for a meeting with a senior lawyer. As I waited in reception, I pondered what had brought me here. Philip, a businessman I knew, had made the introduction suggesting we connect as Christian lawyers. I was not sure what to expect.

An hour later, Paul, the lawyer, and I were deep in conversation. I was fascinated to hear how he and his partners had grown a sizeable law-firm based on a Christian ethos, about the work they undertook, and the varied causes he was involved in beyond the firm. In turn, I recounted my story in law, brief spell in HR, and eagerness to be effective as a Christian in the marketplace.

But just as things were coming to a close, the meeting turned in a direction I was not expecting.

'Would you consider working for us?' Paul asked with a warm smile.

Taken aback, I somewhat awkwardly answered, 'Oh gosh, I hope you haven't misunderstood me. Philip suggested we meet because of our common interests. But I wasn't asking for a job.' I did, of course, need one but that was not the purpose of the meeting.

'No, I haven't misunderstood,' he replied, still smiling, 'but I'd like you to consider joining us.'

'My goodness...' I blustered, my face no doubt reflecting the surprise of my mind. 'Of course, I'm really interested and have loved hearing about the firm. But you've caught me off-guard. Can I have a few days to think about it?' I answered.

'Of course. Why don't we speak on Friday?' came his rely.

And so began a process of considering. Working as a lawyer exclusively again had not been on my horizon - I had been thinking of the world of HR. But in spite of my surprise, I had to wonder if this could be God's provision for me, especially as I had not been looking for it. Still, I had questions: did I have the right legal experience for the firm, could I work in its London office, were the other partners as keen to have me? But as each was satisfactorily answered, I sensed this was my next step. Remarkably within a few weeks it was settled. I was to join the firm as a solicitor.

Given this opportunity arose only months after the big MS relapse, I found myself yet again in awe at God's hand on my life. It had all happened so quickly. Just eight weeks earlier, I had visited my friend, Debs, relaying the sudden loss of head-hunter interest in me and barrier MS now appeared to be in my job search. The memory of that catch up is still fresh in my mind. We sat in a field beside her home, absorbing the peace and beauty that unspoiled nature pours over even troubled hearts. And mine was that day. But Debs was undeterred. Reminding me that God always had, she prayed He would show His goodness in my life; that a door would open and an opportunity arise, not knowing how that could happen. But now it appeared it had in this entirely unexpected way.

Happily, the new job ticked several 'ideal fit' boxes for me. There was parking at its London office, the firm's values aligned with my own, and the partners agreed to my working four rather than five days a week leaving valuable time for other pursuits.

But it was not without significant challenge. Because walking and movement were now more difficult, I was in unchartered territory in terms of what that might feel like at work. Before joining I was entirely honest with the partners about my journey explaining that despite its pressures MS had not impeded my progress at work. And I was open about the relapse too - that it was the first of note in my history but I was still optimistic my health would resettle.

As soon as I joined the firm, however, I could feel the increased physical demand. Initially the offices were in the Gray's Inn building. Delightful from an historical point of view but an obstacle course for me as I tried to negotiate uneven pavements, steep stairs, and meandering interiors.

There was also a strong sense of déjà vu back to my trainee days when I struggled with functioning at work while trying to keep

MS in the background of my story. Fourteen years on, the disease was now more advanced, the pressure more intense. Even the shortest walk felt quite tortuous as I leant heavily on a stick to support my weaker legs.

People were also more obviously taken aback by me on an initial introduction which took me by surprise; a case of Jennifer on the inside forgetting that Jennifer on the outside looks different. That is not by way of criticism. I could see that 'smiling, chatty Jennifer' in the guise of solicitor on the one hand and 'frail, struggling to walk Jennifer' on the other was a perplexing combination. But just as in the past I assumed an upbeat tone with others so MS was not the first thing they thought about in relation to me, I did again. Overall, I think it worked.

But even with the best planning to avoid difficult situations, there were times that was not possible with painful results. One such occasion was at court outside London. At the end of the day, a local lawyer offered to walk my colleague and I to a nearby restaurant for dinner. When I proposed getting a taxi, he suggested that wouldn't be necessary or indeed possible as it was 'only a minute away'. Of course, put like that, I felt obliged to acquiesce but found, as I often did, that a minute away was really ten to me and far too much to cope with in the strong July heat. (Heat can be hugely debilitating for people with MS and was for me.) As a result, we walked at snail's pace, my stress and increasing embarrassment obvious as I tried to chat pretending everything was fine. But it was clear to all it was not. Inwardly I berated myself for not insisting on a taxi. I should have known better than to put myself through this. I fought the urge to cry.

Thankfully this kind of episode was not the norm. Most of the time I was in the office which meant the good times at the firm were many and far outweighed the difficult. I loved my colleagues, the clients (most of the time!), and the interesting work we did.

Fast forward a year, however, and I was forced to a devastating discovery. In spite of my hope that I wouldn't, I was continuing to deteriorate. MS was no longer confined in my body as it had been. That put me in a new MS phase called secondary progressive, essentially 'downhill from here' although medics would not put it so bluntly. I was horrified. It was not dramatic or noticeable day to day but subtle and unrelenting. Now what would the future hold?

Because I am naturally a fighter, I continued working at the firm for another three years. There wasn't a reason to stop as I was able to do my job, though I had to battle to bring my best to work while resisting the inward demoralisation of decline. But in spite of the challenges, I managed. In fact, I managed well.

Now looking back at my professional life, I like to think it broke some barriers in terms of perceptions of people with disabilities at work. I was fortunate to be given opportunity to do that by all my employers but, particularly to its credit, the latter firm which hired me when MS was most obvious. I hope the partners know how deeply appreciative I was.

But with this health discovery came the realisation I needed a major internal reset to survive. **Misery or joy going forwards would depend on the life of my heart.**

A conversation a few months after the relapse proved defining, a huge signpost from God about how to navigate the future. At church a girl I did not know terribly well came to ask how I was seeing my altered walk. I proceeded to tell her my woes and how disappointed I was that my health was worse. The following Sunday, she approached me again. To my surprise, she told me she had sensed God saying that in this time of greater difficulty I needed to 'mine deeply for treasure in God'. Although I smiled and thanked her, inside I was annoyed. I had been expecting God to pat me on the shoulder saying He understood how tough life was but to hold on because healing was on its way or words to that effect. Instead, He apparently had not mentioned healing, offered no sympathy, and instead was asking me to dig deeper into His heart.

But when I pondered her words with a cooler head, I had to admit to knowing they were God's. I also knew this was a critical moment of response for me. God was telling me that the best navigation tool for this time was to have an even deeper and closer relationship with Him and His Word. If I did, the promise was I would find treasure, which I knew was the treasure of knowing Him more and its inevitable transformative effect on my life.

Because I know how weak and foolish I can be, I was surprised to find myself accepting the invitation quickly. But life had shown me by now that the cost of ignoring God's invitation was certain to be too high. I had tasted the sour fruit of my own flawed wisdom enough times in the past. I determined therefore to be intentional, ruthless even, in chasing after God. If there was treasure to be found, I wanted the biggest cache to be had.

Which begs the question, what did that look like? Essentially, it meant having a whole new level of resolve to fix my eyes on

Jesus - an 'Advanced Bootcamp'. I call it that because it was a major step up from the levels of discipline in mind and heart thinking I had previously adopted. Like a regular soldier promoted to the Marines, the bar was now newly set around content in my inner world if I was to thrive in the face of diminishing health.

My new habit had to be a continual gaze on Jesus and the truths He embodied. To do that, I needed to narrow my focus like a soldier on the front line who leaves the noise of life behind to concentrate fully on winning the battle.

To sustain this inward Jesus-gaze, I repeatedly brought to mind truth contained in Him, for example that He loved me, that He would make a way in my wilderness, and that I was a powerful person with choice. I needed to saturate my mind with life-giving thoughts even when circumstances screamed at me to believe the opposite. They often did, especially when I saw further decline.

I aimed at what I called the 'never line', *never* allowing myself to linger in emotional darkness. That meant I had to refuse the barrage of negative thoughts that came like an assault, whispering things were now far worse justifying complaints of, 'Why is this happening God?', 'Are my hopes or dreams possible?', 'Is healing really coming?'.

I needed to remind myself I was in a full-on battle. And I needed to go back to the wisdom of the Word which said the enemy would flee if I submitted to God and resisted him. Despite now being in far heavier combat, I was delighted to discover it remained true. The sword of the Word was powerful heavy artillery and effective regardless of the intensity of war.

In terms of upping my game, I increased my practice of familiar habits such as memorising Scriptures to rebut negative thinking. In my health angst, I also ran to Jesus with new hunger and vulnerability to find my daily nourishment. I needed to know His love even more deeply to overcome what was in front of me. Paul writes that we can be filled to the measure of all the fullness of God[24] – a staggering claim. And while I knew I had some way to go in living in this measure of God's fullness, I knew that had to be my pursuit.

New strategies I adopted made a big difference as well. I got a personal physical trainer for the first time and began to exercise regularly. It was transformative, not only having someone help me improve the limited function I had but a boost to my morale as I did something to help myself. In tandem with that, I made changes to my diet. I had never eaten badly but I began to be more rigorous about avoiding sugary and processed foods on top of increasing the volume of fresh food. I even became an avid greens juicer aware that what goes into my body must affect my health. Happily, what began out of fear is now something I love; I cannot imagine not exercising and eating really well.

I also recognised the importance of living in the present and not becoming fixated on MS or the promise of healing. I had learned to my cost that it is a mistake to be so forward focused that we miss the present. Living fully in, and being thankful for now, is often a necessary steppingstone to receiving the promise as God carves character on the way. In many contexts, such as a meal with friends, having MS made no difference to my fun. But I had to choose to see it that way. I also knew it would be wrong to fixate on healing in the belief life would somehow be perfect when it came. It wouldn't because life isn't. So, aware I had often missed the moment in my tantrum years, I determined to squeeze all the goodness I could out of this season tough or not.

But my biggest win in this time was building internal strength so I was not utterly emotionally derailed when MS was most exposed and difficult. *This was huge.*

For example, on the days I forgot to bring my own, I dreaded the excursion for a lunchtime sandwich even more than I had. As I walked to a café, I would stare tensely at the uneven pavement telling my right leg to lift as it barely could. In a brave moment I would look up, surprised at how many people's eyes I would catch. Why were they looking at me, always at my face and not my leg? I guess I must have been an unusual sight, a youngish (!) woman in a suit, clearly in the working world and yet struggling to walk. In earlier years, these were my worst moments of despair even though I walked better. But in this harder season, I knew I simply could not let that happen.

So, I changed my self-talk. With every tentative step, inwardly I repeated positive statements, for example that Jesus was my Help, that MS had to leave my body because Jesus defeated sickness on the cross, and that God's joy was my strength. It was a battle, but by the time I walked back to the office my inner world had invariably became stronger and more hopeful as I reminded myself of truth in the face of physical pressures. Getting to that point took enormous emotional and determined effort. But over time I was pleased to see the fragile Jennifer on the outside becoming tough as nails on the inside as I stubbornly reinforced the habit of shutting the door on thoughts that were not life giving.

As I applied this approach to every situation which offered the choice of despair over hope, a hope-filled mindset became almost habitual. It seemed to emit both in my being and what I said. To my surprise, people increasingly commented on it until finally the eureka moment came. *This was how the treasure was showing up in my life!*

Truthfully, the Advanced Bootcamp battles wrought the biggest change in me of my whole journey simply because the pressure of coping with progressing MS and working life was so enormous. But even though this battlefield was the toughest, I never felt as close to defeat as in the early days. I guess I had learned better how to journey with God to receive what I needed one day at a time. And when I did, I was never disappointed; love, hope, and joy to a greater extent than ever before it seemed had taken up residence in me.

That is not to say, of course, that I did not have bad days or feel negative emotions. That would not be honest or, indeed, healthy emotionally. Life still happened and, like everyone else, sometimes I needed to feel the hard stuff to get to the other side of pain. But I had found a life-map with the route to a safe place whenever I felt weak. That meant that for every difficulty, whether MS related or not, there was an intersection I always came to. At the intersection, I would pause and process whatever was going on. But after a time, a choice had to be made. To go forward on the road of introspection and heaviness with Jesus at a distance because I would not take His hand, or to go forward on the road of hope with Jesus near as I held His outstretched hand. Over the years I had learned that, while we can't always control what happens to us, we can choose our response. And I had by now concluded that the better road was always the latter.

But a humorous moment from this season stands out. Away for a weekend with friends, one of them, Sophie, greeted me on Sunday telling me how radiant I looked. As I am just as susceptible to savouring a compliment as the next person, I privately basked in her words as I headed back to my hotel room.

Absorbed in my own thoughts, I was suddenly interrupted by the sound of a little girl's voice and the question, 'Are you VERY OLD?' Lifting my head I saw a little girl approaching, perhaps age six but could not see the elderly person she was talking to. It took a moment for me to compute - she was talking to me! I suppose she thought I was very old because of my slow walk with a stick but I wasn't quite expecting to be put into that category in my forties…

After a moment puzzling how to answer, I heard myself say, 'I'm not very, very old but I am middling old', which seemed to satisfy her as she skipped away.

Although suitably brought back to earth with a bang the humour of the exchange was not lost on me; from the heights of radiant to depths of 'very old' within minutes.

Proof, I guess, that even in the toughest seasons there are things to make us smile!

Notes

[24] Ephesians 3:19

17

ABOVE GROUND

Even the darkest night will end and the sun will rise.
Victor Hugo

This brings me to a chapter I was particularly excited to write. That's because I get to describe what happened when the cumulative gains from my journey - changed thinking and depths in hope and joy - began to appear. I knew it was real because, to my surprise, life met me in a totally different way.

With re-formed responses, I was living *with* Jesus far more than only running to Him in need. Among other things, I stepped into a measure of heart healing I was not expecting. Things which had hurt sharply in the past such as the loss of a music career and grief over MS, began not to hurt. It was as if pieces of splintered glass were being removed from within.

This led me to a richer place in my heart than I had ever known; like being in a garden and walking on pavements of heaven's qualities such as gentleness, faithfulness, and peace. It lent itself to better emotional health because the pathways oozed the wholeness of heaven. When the storms of life hit, as they inevitably did, I was newly protected from their havoc as I learned to walk on and in God's heart.

But the contrast between the road I travelled to get me there and the beauty of the destination was not lost on me. It was the loss and pain of a journey with MS that had pushed me to dig for the treasure of life entwined in Jesus' love. Yet this contrast is intrinsic to the Christian life. The suffering and death of Jesus became the soil of resurrection and redemption for humankind. The seeming contradiction of dying preceding living.

Given these internal changes, perhaps I should have expected an external impact too. But I did not.

The earliest clue was when I noticed my interactions with people were different. At first, I was simply nicer. For example, in the past at a store counter I would have paid and gone on my way, absorbed in my own world. But more and more, love seemed to want to stand up in me to lean out and touch those in my path. Like water in a jug which overflows when an object is placed in it, my self-focus was being displaced by Jesus in me. The only thing I was doing was yielding to Him, but the unexpected result was Him being much more active through me.

Increasingly I could not help myself lingering to chat to assistants at paying tills which often became my prophesying over them, offering an insight from God or praying for them. I never planned these exchanges but was amazed as, time after time, I left with a story of someone touched by God's love.

I remember Nina at Sainsbury's checkout with a bandage around her wrist. When I asked what happened and offered to pray, she readily accepted although was slightly surprised when I did so on the spot. We did not have much time as a queue formed behind me. But she thanked me profusely as I finished, telling me she would be there the following Friday and hoped to see me. When I went back a week later to give her a short book about Jesus, she told me she had been waiting all week for my return. A lesson to me that we foolishly pay homage to fear of man when people are desperate for the light every believer carries. I do not know the end of her story, but I sowed seeds - God will do the rest.

I should have guessed, however, that in heaven's 'never-ending-ness', Jesus was not going to stop there. He began to stretch me farther, (more courage required…), nudging me to offer insights to people I came across like a barista in a coffee shop, the workmen who came to do home repairs, and even people I spoke to in call centres.

Once while slightly bored on hold to a call centre, I asked God if he had anything to say to the gentleman who was helping me. I have often thought it must be a horribly tedious job dealing with demanding customers.

'Yes', came God's answer; 'Thomas has sacrificed a lot for a dependant family member with special needs, and I want you to tell him I have seen his sacrifice and am about to make a way for him to do things he put aside for his family.' I have found it is not difficult to be brave at the end of a 'phone so, once my enquiry was dealt with and he asked if there was anything else he could help me with (they always do), I told him there was – I just needed a few minutes of his time. I proceeded to tell him I was a Christian, had heard God speak about him, and asked if he would like to hear what He said. Odd though it sounds even describing that dialogue on paper, generally I find people quick to assess if they are dealing with a sensible human being or not which, of course, guides their answer. I must have passed the sensibleness test as he immediately asked me to continue. To say he was moved and floored by what I said would be a huge understatement. With amazement in his voice, he told me his son was autistic and that there were many things he had not been able to do in life in order to look after him. I could hear him fighting tears as he told me the sacrifice point was spot on. I was equally moved. What a difference the word must have made to him. Perhaps he was at the end of his tether that day? Perhaps he had given up on his dreams? Perhaps he had never known there was a God who saw him? Whatever his thoughts or need, that day he got to hear loud and clear that God loved him and had a better future for him. And all through a random stranger crossing his path (or phoneline!).

I was always amazed and touched by the impact. People almost never objected to hearing and, if there was initial scepticism, I would see it dissolve as they acknowledged the accuracy of the message. They were nearly always blown away that God knew them so well and sent a stranger to 'show and tell' of His love.

Another particularly memorable encounter took place at Starbucks. On the day, the café was very busy and I was wrapped up in my own world listening to music while on my laptop. A woman with a young baby tapped me on the shoulder asking if she could join me at my table. Once I had smiled yes, I put my earphones back in. But within seconds, I felt that familiar inner nudge of God getting my attention. I heard Him speaking about the woman and her baby, so grabbed a piece of paper to write what He said. Although they were wonderfully encouraging words, I did wonder with some nervousness how I was going to open a conversation to deliver them.

Experience, however, had shown me that being direct was often the best approach, so I leant across the table to say, 'Excuse me for interrupting but I am a Christian. I believe that God speaks today and, just now, have felt Him say some things He would like me to tell you.' My voice trailed off somewhat as I looked at her face, reserved to say the least. But smiling I went on. 'God has encouraging things to say. Would you like to hear?' To my relief, she nodded yes.

I then began to tell her what God had said, numerous things but, particularly, that He wanted her to know she was a great Mum at which point I saw her eyes well up with tears. I kept going, however, so she got it all. Once I finished, there was a slightly awkward pause.

'Does that make any sense to you?' I asked. Her answer astounded me.

'This morning I was at the hospital with my baby, Grace, and given really bad news about her health. I went to a park afterwards and said to God, 'God, if you are really there, now is a good time to tell me.' Then I came here for coffee and you just told me God has spoken to you about us. Not only that, but I was beating myself up for being such a useless Mum, partly to blame for Grace's problems. I can't believe what you have just said.' I had also spoken about who her baby would be as she grew up and God's plans for her life, not knowing anything about her bad health.

We were both a bit shell-shocked. She, no doubt, because God had just answered her prayer in a remarkable way and I, because I knew I had nearly disobeyed God's prompt to speak to her for fear of being rebuffed.

As the baby began to cry, she got up to leave but I asked Emily, (we were on first name terms by now,) if she would let me pray for Grace quickly. She agreed so I put my hand on Grace's tummy intent on keeping it short saying, 'Jesus, I release healing over Grace.' and that was it. As she left, her parting comment was that she recognised me from the gym - I was a regular at the one nearby.

But I was amazed by the encounter. In awe of how God, knowing Emily's pain, had set events up so she would run into someone in a café who would give her reason to hope after she asked Him to speak to her. Not only that, but that the person would also tell her that her baby would live as I had prophesied about Grace's future. A strong reminder too that I needed to respond to God's prompts because, if I did not, someone could be deprived of life-changing encouragement they desperately needed.

If that had been the end of the story it would have been great, but it wasn't.

In the gym about six weeks later, a girl approached me asking, 'Do you want to know what happened?' For a few moments I looked at her blankly before recognising Emily from Starbucks.

'Oh hello, I didn't recognise you at first. Of course, I'd love to hear!' I replied. Emily went on, 'Well, since the day you prayed for Grace, she has been completely well.'

Amazed (I know I shouldn't have been…) I asked, 'You mean no disease at all?'

'Yes,' came the reply at which point we both broke into a huge grin and gave each other a hug! The funny thing in the moment was that we were both with personal trainers who were looking on in bewilderment at their clients hugging. Of course, I relayed the whole story to mine after.

Fast forward two years when I ran into Emily again in the gym, not having seen her in the interim. She pointed to a beautiful little toddler running around, saying, 'That's Grace, look at her now.' Even recalling the story makes me want to weep. I could only rejoice at the miracle in front of my eyes with her mum.

But I will admit there is some puzzling irony to Grace being healed but not me by then, a fact that was not lost on Emily who saw my difficulty walking. Didn't I get people to pray for me like I had Grace, she enquired, as she tried to make sense of her daughter's healing against the obvious lack of mine.

Perplexing I agree, and I have had to wrestle that mystery about my healing with God. After all, if God's heart is always to heal, why was I still waiting for it? More broadly, why do some wait longer for their healing breakthrough than others or, indeed, not see it at all? Valid questions worthy of more comment than these chapters allow and on which there are a number of excellent books. But as my chief anchor point on the subject, I have learned I must never move away from what the Bible teaches about healing even if my experience does not always perfectly reflect it.

I am a work in progress in every respect in my walk with God which means, while I would love to see every person I pray for immediately healed, I refuse to lose heart if they are not. That would be letting experience prevail over truth. Although I believe complete healing is available now, Jesus Himself indicated some progressive growth would be involved in His children doing greater works than He beyond His earthly lifetime (John 14:12). Putting what I may not understand aside, I am committed to that growth journey. In the meantime, I keep truth firmly in front of me knowing God's heart is always to heal, and that trusting Him is the only posture of heart safety. In doing so, I keep the door wide open to increasingly being His conduit for healing and experiencing it myself.

Because I hate, no, actually detest disease and its effects, I would take almost every opportunity I could to pray for healing for anyone in need. I felt so full of God in this season that I had an ease and boldness about doing so. I soon saw this generally confounded people, like it had Emily, perhaps because, in their eyes, the notion of someone like me with obvious health difficulties praying for healing for someone else was oxymoron-like. But I saw it differently.

I remember Ian, a security guard at work who struggled to walk with painful hips. He used to see me coming to work limping myself and, after some weeks of warm greetings, he agreed to let me pray for him. As we talked about Jesus, he asked me why I was praying for him and not for me. The 'me first' world we live in is not expecting the servanthood Jesus so perfectly lived of loving others even when we have needs ourselves. But consider that Jesus ministered to the man crucified with Him despite His own agony at the time. In my case, my need is obvious. Yours might not be, a broken heart, addiction, finance pressures, loneliness, but is equally valid, maybe worse than mine. But in my own place of need, every time I pray for someone it is an act of warfare against the enemy who would like me to be demoralised and out of active service for God. I am neither. Because I have choice, I refuse to be consumed by my own concerns and prevented from partnering with God to release His Kingdom around me. It would be my loss entirely to miss out on the joy that comes when I do. And even when little appears to happen, I remind myself that something always happens when I pray.

Once I prayed seemingly unremarkably for a workman from overseas at my home. Yet just a few hours later I was amazed to get a tearful call from his wife who rang to thank me, so touched she said that someone had done so. They had been having a difficult time settling in the UK and were hugely comforted that God had had someone reach out to them. You just never know the difference it makes.

Yet even when I did not reach out to people, in this season it seemed like the world reached out to me. It was as if I had become a magnet for kindness, which only increased the more fragile I appeared. To function in life, I now often needed to ask strangers for help, such as asking for the arm of a passing City worker to walk the very short walk from my car to workplace or a passer-by to help me across the road.

After some surprise at my approach, generally people's responses were wonderful. Invariably, they could not do enough for me and disrupted their days to help. My nature is to be warm and chatty. I sensed my normality took them aback a little, perhaps not what they expected in someone struggling to walk. But the loveliness of these exchanges never ceased to amaze me, people almost glowing at my thanks for their kindness, the best in their hearts rising towards me as they seemingly relished the chance to be helpful. Perhaps therein is a lesson for us. Is it that humanity is aching to be needed, appreciated, greeted by warmth? If we would only call out the best in people, would we see it more?

Something else I noticed in this time was people wanting to draw from me. I began to see it in all kinds of situations - after preaching at church, in small talk with strangers, and with colleagues at work. I was being invited for more coffees than I could manage! Puzzled, I asked God what was happening. To my surprise, He told me people were trying to draw from my well of hope, joy, and passion for Jesus. Although I did not see myself in those terms, I guess it proved that heaven's atmosphere is a magnet to the world. People really are hungry for true hope and joy and not the fake the world offers. And once I understood that, it only increased my boldness to talk about Jesus wherever I could. Simple warmth and a smile seemed to open doors of conversation easily and frequently, although I was in no doubt the most powerful moments of God stepping in to touch someone were always entirely orchestrated by Him.

Being frank, I used to think one meaningful exchange with someone each month or week was a good 'Christian record' if there is such a thing. But I began to see that every contact with a person is God's invitation to us to make His fingerprints visible. And I found to the extent I was willing, I began to have these encounters almost every day, even multiple times a day. I cannot say I seized every opportunity - fear of rejection still lurked in the background - but when I ignored my fears, God always reached out.

In fact, God would even reach out when I was not in a cooperative frame of mind. I recall Mark, a young cab driver, telling me about his agonising back pain as he drove me home. I was tired after the working day and not inclined to chat. But as Mark drove, I kept getting a picture in my mind's eye of a medieval jester. For a while I ignored it reminding God I was tired. But as it persisted and I realised God was not bothered by my tiredness, I asked Him what it meant. Delightfully I heard Him say Mark was really funny and He wanted to encourage him to use his gift of humour as a comedian; an entirely new concept of calling to me. As I told Mark, I could see his eyes enlarge with astonishment in the rear-view mirror before he told me he was considering leaving cab driving to become a comedian! Then it was my turn to be amazed at God's intersection of our lives so Mark would hear God's message for him at just the right time. But there's more.

When we arrived at my house, I offered to pray for his back. It was brief - 'Lord, I loose healing over Mark's back.' To his incredulity he said heat went through his body and the pain immediately left. That day he did not give his life to Jesus but he did get introduced to Him in a powerful way, as God showed him how much He loved him celebrating his humour and restoring his health. I came away only invigorated and joyful, and reminded again of why I should never hold back and miss the opportunity to be a part of releasing heaven on earth.

Something else unexpected was the encouragement people seemed to draw from my life on occasion. For instance, a young trainer at the gym told me he sometimes felt depressed when he came. But if he saw me, he would think about the effort it had taken me to get there which then motivated him to exercise and shake off his heaviness. I had no idea this young man struggled with depression but was even more amazed that my feeble efforts to strengthen my legs had an effect on anyone at all. But this was just one of many times people would say things like that to me.

My point is absolutely not that I am inspirational - I never feel that - but that our doing and being in life in spite of our circumstances can impact people for the good in ways we never imagine and without us even uttering a word.

Eventually, I recognised my arrival at a stage of such change that the fist I once held up in anger at life had become a smile. My perspective had undergone a 360° turn which meant my default was joyful and thankful most of the time. If you had seen how angry and miserable I was in those early years, you would know that was a miracle.

But I knew the secret of this place I had come to was my finding true life in Jesus. That is the connection that releases heaven's charge of love and, from that, everything necessary to deal with life circumstances. This is a wonderful place. When intimacy with God is first, it is like being part of the roots of a tree nourished directly from the soil of God's heart. Then when different seasons come, whether pruning and clearing or budding and blooming, our access to God is the same so we can continually be nourished by Him.

From the time of deciding to go deeper with God until today, my priority has been that deeper pursuit. At times, I would experience such wonderful connectedness to God I would want to bottle and hand it out to others.

Friends would often ask me how I found these places of encounter. My best answer was that hunger for God is key.

The Bible promises that we will find God if we seek Him with all our hearts, and that He rewards those who diligently search for Him. In a sense, therefore, we bear some responsibility for the richness of the table we sit at with God because we decide how earnestly we pursue Him. That isn't a wearisome pursuit but the eagerness of a lover for her beloved. Yet the opposite is also true. We come to the table with nothing but appetite; God serves us the richest meal. We can only love Him because He first loved us which means He is the source of the love we grow deeper in and then offer back to Him as we allow our hunger to draw us towards Him. But look at the power of our hunger,

> '*Then suddenly my longings transported me. My divine desire brought me next to my beloved prince, sitting with him in his royal chariot....*' (Song of Songs 6:12 TPT)

Who would not want to let longing be stirred with that promise of its affect?

Above all, I remind myself no one else can go deeper in God for me - I must do that myself. Although I value my incredible friends more than I can say, I have long known that my most treasured time in life is time alone with my King. I am ruined for anything else and not ashamed of saying so.

Have I seen my own desires fulfilled by now? Yes, some, but many others not yet. I am not married and, while I struggled with that for a time, I don't now. I live in an assurance of God's faithfulness in my life and that He is always doing a new thing. Meanwhile I have been lavished with the best friends and privileged to live in a deep and nourishing awareness of my union with the Bridegroom, Jesus. It is my delight; a prize above all else. God never short-changes us.

I am also clear much of my life to date has been preparation for the future and am so appreciative of what has filled it thus far, not least time as a musician, lawyer, church leader, prophet, and preacher. And in recent years I have added training as a life coach to that collection, helping people become unstuck in life so they can live freely towards their best.

I know the enemy tried to use MS to cripple my life, inwardly and outwardly, but God has used it as a doorway to fashion my heart and thinking for His best. As He often reminds me, I am only at the threshold of stepping into it all:

> *'Things never discovered or heard of before,*
> *things beyond our ability to imagine these are*
> *are the many things God has in store for all his*
> *lovers. But God now unveils these profound*
> *realities to us by the Spirit.'* (1 Corinthians 2:9-10 TPT)

I can't wait!

18

WEIGHT OF THE WAIT

I can be changed by what happens to me.
But I refuse to be reduced by it.
Mayo Angelou

In terms of my expected healing, you may wonder if people prayed for me to be healed over the years. Yes, they did; often. However apart from the dramatic partial healing of that first year, I never saw visible physical improvement. In the early years that was often crushing as my view of a better future was so wrapped up in being healed. But as the years passed with God teaching me what true hope and fullness of life really were, I came to a much better place.

I also learned it is impossible for nothing to happen when someone prays because God always responds to faith. After all, it was He who urged us to ask to receive from Him. With that understanding then, when people prayed for me, I began to aim at always expecting something extraordinary to happen but not being discouraged if it did not.

That said, the waiting has not been without cost. Its weight was agonising at times.

With hindsight I see it in two parts. To borrow an earlier metaphor, it was bitter for a long time as I struggled against learning the things God wanted to teach me. Only when I did, did I begin to taste its sweetness, not in the distress of sickness of course, but out of the place of friendship with God I found.

Much of this learning came out of the life of Abraham which God directed me to read again and again. I could see the parallels in our journeys. The first patriarch in the Bible, God called Abraham to leave his land for one He promised to give him. He also promised him many descendants who would bless the nations of the world – all this when Abraham and his wife Sarah were childless! But what unfolds in his story is a wait of twenty-five years to see the promise of a son fulfilled amidst a description of the many mistakes he made on the way.

My first lesson was around the cycle of mistrust and trust I would yo-yo between about God fulfilling His promise of healing to me as the years went by. Often, I was angry at it taking so long and would doubt God's intent to heal. As I have described, negativity would then flood my life leading me on a downward spiral. But repeatedly God pointed to Abraham's story to show me a lengthy wait did not mean God would not be faithful. Just as He had done everything He promised in Abraham's life, so He would in mine. But first I had to let go of my petulant attitude which was trying to force God's hand to act. So did Abraham. In his case, he tried to self-fulfil God's promise to him by having a child with his servant girl. But only after the child's arrival and God repeating that

His promise would not come through that son, did he finally offer a fully yielded heart to God.

In my case the root of my demanding mindset was also an un-yielded heart. Unfortunately for me, I did not learn quickly. I had seasons of yielding only to pick up my anger at God again. It was not until I finally gave all my demands up asking for His way or no way that I found the stability and peace I craved as I chose to trust God in the waiting.

The second lesson was learning the tenacity of holding onto God's promises regardless of contrary circumstances or the views of others. When we know God has spoken, we need to be able to maintain a consistent belief in His promise. Doubtless when God first spoke to Abraham, he told his family excitedly of God's promise to give him a son, and a huge clan, as he persuaded them to leave their home. Yet with the passing years he must have faced ridicule as he and Sarah aged without bearing a child.

To remain confident in the face of undermining from others takes real spiritual stamina and yet is necessary in holding out for the promise of God. So just as Abraham had to, I saw God developing the same kind of resilience in me, one which was not undermined by my physical deterioration or the incredulity of others for believing, in their minds, the fantasy that I would be healed. In the early years I was far too easily buffeted by these things but, as I matured into deeper friendship with God, I became steadier. After all, He had shown me His great power at work at that conference in the first year of MS. Was I going to believe Him, the God of the impossible, or medics whose knowledge was less than God's power or the unbelief of others?

Over time the Jennifer whose professed belief in healing was somewhat changeable in the early years became fierce and immoveable in her trust God would heal her. Even better I reached a stage when I actually did not care what other people thought in terms of not letting their beliefs undermine mine. My heart eyes were set on God and what He told me, and in that place, more and more, it was my faith I would see set the faith temperature in whatever context I found myself.

The third lesson was around God's kindness in vulnerability; His stooping down to help us when we struggle to believe. Scripture makes clear the fulfilment of every promise will be tested and waiting is surely one of the toughest tests. It is so easy for doubt to creep in when memory of first hearing God's voice begins to fade and we wonder whether He will do what may seem impossible.

For Abraham, he faced repeated disappointment at the ongoing failure of him and his wife to conceive. But while we see him hitting rock bottom moments of doubt along the way, we also see God's extraordinary kindness towards him. More than once, God appears to him, repeating and expanding on His promise and even once turning up with two angels to eat with him to reinforce the point![25] That only confirmed to me I could go back to God for similar reassurance when I had my own weak moments, like the bruising trainee day in chapter 5 when my hope ran out. Then when I turned to God, He repeated His promise telling me He would make my footsteps firm.

Of course, I still needed to learn to grow my muscles of trust in believing His promise day to day but that did not mean God wouldn't put His arm round me to encourage me when I needed. Interestingly later in Romans 4, we read that Abraham did not 'waver in unbelief' but remained confident that regardless of he and his wife's advanced ages God would be faithful to His promise. While we see moments of doubt in the Genesis account of Abraham's life, perhaps what Paul is describing here is the place of faith and doubt we can experience in tension, like the man who came to Jesus saying, *'I do believe; help my unbelief'* (Mark 9:23-25).

In the deep places within me, I do not think I ever doubted God's promise to heal me but there were moments when doubt and fear would creep into the upper floors of my heart so to speak. Looking at Abraham's life I saw I was not alone in this but, like him my need never allowed them to overtake my deeper conviction that God would be faithful to me.

Until I got through learning those lessons the weight of the wait was as bitter as I have said. But when I started to embrace the learning, I began to taste sweetness. What I mean is that having dived into the deep places God led me of hope, joy, and Advanced Bootcamp, the good changes I have described began to appear. The heaviness of the wait in resisting God and accompanying misery was replaced by increasing lightness with heart eyes joyfully fixed on God.

I can see now that the length of the wait bore immense fruit in reshaping my heart. It developed considerable perseverance and endurance, qualities perhaps less popular today than ever before as society lauds speed and instant results. But in heaven's workshop, these qualities are not optional. When our faith is tested and endurance fully developed, the Bible tells us we will be perfect and complete, needing nothing[26]. The hour we live in is critical. Even the most casual observation of world events confirms our urgent need of endurance and perseverance. We must choose the ways of God to grow in them to become strong and mature, fully equipped for the times ahead.

When we see Abraham at the latter part of his waiting journey we read that he *'grew strong in faith........ being fully assured that what God had promised, He was able also to perform.'* (Romans 4:20-21). I can honestly say the longer I have waited, the stronger in persevering trust my faith has become.

I could not have imagined the waiting would yield what it has – the happy fruit of trust, hope, and deep friendship with God.

It is not a popular message, but it is true; what is sculpted in us through the waiting we could not learn any other way.

Notes

[25] Genesis 18:1-15

[26] James 1:2-3 NLT

19

GREAT EXPECTATIONS!

Grow out of your innermost selves
Never renounce your beliefs
Do not toil for recognition
But always do all you can so that
the field allotted to you may prosper
Leoš Janáček

Now you have read the journey, perhaps I can offer some thoughts.

As I stated in the introduction, I wrote this book to tell people there is a measure of hope and joy available in God which will not only be a firm foundation for meaningful life but will sustain them through life's greatest hardships. These are not the only aspects of His nature we need but, in my journey, I have found them to be critical pillars in keeping my house (me) from collapse in the most difficult times. Now having tasted these gems, I am dismayed to see many living in hopelessness and joylessness to varying degrees, both believers and non-believers. Of course, life will present hopeless and joyless moments to us all. But I have learned that the bleak message they carry does not have to be the prevailing wind in our lives.

This is the truth - we have a loving Father who offers all that we need through His Son, so we can walk in light and not darkness. Hopelessness is darkness; no looking upwards or outwards; a lifeless existence. But with hope there is a heartbeat which allows the many other good things we need to enter, not least joy, that great dispeller of heaviness. These are key ingredients in the recipe for a healthy mind and heart.

In saying this, I don't claim to be an expert. I am still learning and speak only from my journey. But its bumps have been sufficiently hard and brought me sufficiently low to know that the hope and joy I found are necessary for fullness of life.

And from that place of discovery and recovery in my own life, if it is not already obvious, I now have great expectation for the future! I am living life well with a smile in spite of MS and its increasing limits. I am also more joyful, hopeful, and in love with Jesus now than I have ever been. There is no end to my delight in the journey of living life enveloped in the One who never ceases to surprise me with His constant newness of touch and conversation. There is no staleness in the relationship or end to His engagement with me, only expansion in the sweetness and potency of His presence. Honestly, most of the time I feel lovesick for Him[27] as He draws me back to encounter Him again and again and again.

At the same time, I live in active anticipation of health being restored. If I needed proof that my belief is real, then I have it on every birthday when, year on year, I find myself genuinely surprised healing is not yet evident in my body. It is not a question of refusing to be content with my reality, but rather settling for contentment would be wrong because I would be denying part of the inheritance Jesus died to give me, which is fullness of health. That has required some head and heart acrobatics on my part to live in joy today despite MS, while actively looking toward the promise of health to come; a posture at times more challenging than accepting the status quo. But I would be denying the truth about God's nature as Healer if I did which means that, tension or not, it is the place of belief I am obliged to occupy.

But there is even better ahead. Just a few years ago when I asked God if He had anything to say to me about healing, much like one might revisit a topic with a friend, He directed me to the story of Aeneas who was paralyzed and bedridden in Acts 9:32-35. In the account, Peter visits him and after saying *'Aeneas, Jesus Christ heals you; get up and make your bed'*, he is immediately completely healed. As I read it, I could sense the fresh breath of God speaking the same promise of restored health to me. But in addition to Aeneas' miracle, God highlighted something else; the fact that two whole cities came to believe in Jesus as a result. I knew He was telling me that my healing would somehow result in substantial impact on others.

Do I ever doubt? A moment in early 2022 post lockdown challenged everything I have said. I set out to revisit my favourite coffee shop in Wandsworth, London, where I used to read and write for hours on end before Covid. Although I had exercised regularly in my house during the pandemic, the space was small, and I did not have my usual gym equipment. What I had not anticipated was the effect the confinement had had on my walking and mobility. As I made my way from car to café, I was shocked to see the immense difficulty I faced, walking slower than before and unable to lift my right leg as I needed. Relieved when I got to the café, I naively did not expect to see any further change. Except there was. Now even walking to the once familiar counter to order was hard as I shuffled, thrown by the café environment. And the kindness of staff in bringing my order to my table despite their queue-only policy spoke volumes about how unsteady I appeared.

When I returned home, I was horribly shaken. It was the worst I had ever seen myself with MS and forced self-examination. Could I still truthfully say I live in the joy, hope, and passion for Jesus I have professed? Did I still believe I would be healed? A telling moment for me.

Yet, as I reflected, I knew the answer was yes. My anchor is Jesus; I remain convinced of the truth about Him regardless of my circumstances. Only He could put those jewels of assurance in my heart when, in the natural, there is plenty of reason to be discouraged. He is the treasure of my life.

Not unreasonably, a question I am sometimes asked is whether I would have dug so deep in God to find the riches I have without MS. I hope I would. I know I did not have to get sickness to find them. Other life challenges would have offered the same invitation to search for and find Him in the process of a trial leading to perseverance, to character, to hope. It is not a 'once for all' learning either. With every life challenge, and plenty come to us all, there is a need for a constant choosing to reach into Jesus for strength and hope to get to the other side of whatever we face and overcome 'it' rather than have 'it' overcome us.

I am conscious too that physical healing when it comes might be slightly anti-climactic, as for a child waiting all year for *the* Christmas gift only to find, when it arrives, it does not bring the absolute life completeness imagined. So, I deliberately do not imagine that it will, although its joy will be magnificent and worthy of great celebration as I have restored to me the ability to move freely and participate in life in ways I have not for a long time. In health terms, it will be 'on earth as it is in heaven' manifested in my life, for which God will get **ALL** the glory with my unbridled delight!! But in the meantime, my hope will continue to be foremost in the person of Jesus and life in Him, not the promise of healing.

Healing aside, as I look at the wider expanse of my life, I am intent on spending the rest of it dreaming with God. I used to think the notion of dreaming was childish and fanciful, but now realise it is essential to really living life as God desires. After all, He dreamt the world into existence by imagining it before creating it. And therein is the blueprint for living – dream or imagine something which establishes purpose and then create it. Everything God does through us is part of His dream life shared with us. How so? Our dreams, the good ones that is, all come from Him as it is He who created us in His image with His life giving us the capacity to dream. We could not have dreamt or imagined apart from Him but are invited to do so with Him, which includes continually expanding our dreams. The Bible describes it like this:

'Now to Him who is able to [carry out His purpose and] do superabundantly more than all that we dare ask or think [infinitely beyond our greatest prayers, hopes, or dreams],

according to His power that is at work within us...'
(Ephesians 3:20 AMP)

For centuries, the church has been bound by the often unspoken, perhaps unconscious belief that God, although loving and limitless in resource, is contradictorily inclined to provide barely enough for our needs and that asking for more is greedy. I certainly believed those falsehoods.

But when I understood who God is, I realised it had to be His desire to release superabundantly more because it is within His nature. Or put another way, how frustrating for God to have to hold back His 'more' because His people do not know or dare to ask for it. Yet His willingness is hardly hidden. Look at the enormity and beauty of the universe. How could we have missed what it shouts to us about the extravagance and generosity of its creator?

I had a particular moment of revelation with God about this. I was asking Him about my own dreams, reminding Him of His promise that if I delighted in Him, He would give me the desire of my heart. It suddenly occurred to me that God Himself must have some wild dreams. I asked Him if He did and, if so, whether I could be part of their fulfilment on earth. It is hard to explain how I felt God immediately become quiet – it was not as if I was hearing His audible voice before I asked the question. But after a pause, in my heart I heard Him answer in changed tone of softness and vulnerability, 'Very few people ask that question.' I could feel He was moved. He told me quietly that He would be delighted to release some of His wildest dreams through me.

Then it was my turn to be quiet. I was undone by His answer, confronted by my own selfishness in having never thought to ask the question before. In prayer I only thought of my own or other people's desires. Since then, my earnest prayer is that my heart be a landing strip for the wildest dreams of heaven, and that He would have the joy of expressing His most wonderful and deep longings through my life. It seems to me that even the possibility of praying in these terms is staggeringly sacred. But, consistent with the outrageously loving heart of heaven, the invitation is there for us all. Yes, I am saying the extent to which we dream with God is actually a matter of our own choosing.

Linked to the boldly dreaming concept, I am fascinated by the examples in the Bible of people who stretched the intentions of heaven because their revelation of God's goodness was such, they knew they could. When we see God responding in kind, delighted by their faith, I am jealously challenged in the best sense to follow suit – these are the radical pioneers!

The centurion who asked Jesus to heal his servant is one such example (Matthew 8:5-13). Jesus readily agreed to come to his house to do so only to have the centurion object, telling Jesus he knew He had the authority to release the miracle simply by speaking it. But what follows is what captivates me. Not only did Jesus tell the listening crowd he was amazed by the faith of the non-Jewish centurion, but He performed the healing exactly as the soldier asked even though it wasn't His original intention. More significant therefore than it being the first remote miracle of His ministry, is that it shows our vision or faith for something can so move God's heart that He will do more than or different to His original plan.

Similarly, we see the 'man's heart moving heaven' principle in the story of Elisha. He was a prophet in training, mentored by the great prophet Elijah. In 2 Kings 2:1-13 we read the story of Elisha's final exchanges with Elijah before God took him up to heaven; he didn't die. Look what happens. Elijah goes on a journey passing through Bethel, Jericho, and Jordan. At each place, he urges Elisha to remain while he travels onwards but Elisha refuses. When they finally pass through the Jordan river, Elijah asks Elisha what he can do for him before he is taken by God. Elisha's request is extraordinary; he asks for a double portion of the spirit of God on Elijah.

It would have been a glorious thing for Elisha to receive exactly the same measure of God working in Elijah's life. Remember, Elijah had called down fire from heaven in his confrontation with the priests of Baal and stopped rain causing famine simply by his words - impressive power. But something stirred in Elisha's heart so he dared ask for a double anointing although there was no precedent in biblical history for his bold request - even Joshua, Moses' successor, did not receive double when he died. Elisha's boldness, therefore, came from a deeper knowing of God's nature.

Helpfully, his journey reveals something of the heart which qualified him to receive his request. At Elijah's urging, Elisha could have stopped at Bethel, the place of intimacy between God and Jacob, asking for an anointing to see and hear; or he could have stopped at Jericho, where walls fell down, asking for a miracle power anointing.

But he refused to settle for less when he knew there was more to be had.

He pressed on to cross the Jordan, symbol of entering the future promised land, to ask for something greater. He was determined to dream with God. In the end, he received that double portion anointing going on to perform many more miracles than Elijah in his life. He received because, knowing the heart and willingness of God, he dreamt it was possible and asked.

There are lessons here which require me to pose two questions. One, do I sufficiently dream with God that my prayers move His heart to do immeasurably more than I could imagine, even things that have never been seen before? Two, like Elisha do I live in such a way to never settle on the journey for less? If I can answer yes to those questions, I give God permission to display an extraordinary measure of His nature on earth, His wildest dreams. The world is desperately in need of them.

Now having seen what God is eager to share of Himself and its unfathomable privilege, I find I simply cannot say no. I have to pursue it, knowing if I do, I will be able to look at God's face seeing His joy at His dreams lived through me.

In conclusion, I am drawn to the film 'Dead Poets Society'. It contains a famous scene in which the late Robin Williams explains the term 'carpe diem' to the students, telling them to make their lives extraordinary. I love that admonition, and my encouragement to anyone reading this is the same.

You are extraordinary, outrageously loved by the God who dreamed you into existence. No one else can make your footprints in the world - they are utterly unique to you. If you do not live your best life, the world will have missed something forever because no one else will bring what you do.

Robin Williams was urging the students to live extraordinary lives through their own efforts which has some merit. But we will never fully step into the extraordinary that we are until we are connected to the Father who created us. Once we are, we become the richest people on the planet, filled with God and able to access His endless resource. This does not mean life will be easy but, without God, we will live in poverty for the lack of knowing His love, forgiveness, and the promise of eternal life. No earthly wealth or experience can come even close to everything available in God and life in Him. If you are in doubt, just think of the tragic ends of the privileged who never found fulfilment in the abundance of the world's offerings.

If we walk with Jesus, we will be on course for a life of love which not only allows us to know our true identity as children of God but will carry us through every difficulty to bring possibility out of seeming impossibility. That is a future and hope. From that place, the footsteps of our lives will carry the deepest imprints of heaven so we can tread extraordinary everywhere we go.

Whatever the destiny or purpose for which God created us, it comes with a unique guarantee. Not only will the extraordinary with God be immeasurably superior to the world's best, but a life lived with God in that way will gain us priceless eternal rewards.

Knowing this leads me to ask a further question. Are you and I prepared to fully offer ourselves for this - a totally abandoned life available to God?

The reasons we do not or cannot may be various; selfishness, independence, fear of inadequacy. Whatever they may be, excuses are puny and powerless in the hands of God whose life in us frees us from ourselves.

He is just waiting for our yes, so He can break the seal on our dreams. He wants to let us loose on the world to live them, being as dangerously brilliant in God as we are created to be; releasing heaven's solutions to an earth desperately in need of His touch.

As He did to Isaiah, God continues to ask, 'Whom shall I send?'

And that is where my journey has taken me, through the lens of all I have described to ask, 'Lord, will you send me?'

Notes

[27] Song of Songs 5:8 *Swear to me, you daughters of Jerusalem, If you find my beloved, As to what you will tell him: For I am lovesick."*

20

MOVEMENT

The people who are crazy enough to think they can change the world are the ones who do.

Steve Jobs

Which takes me full circle to the 'awakened cry in me' I mentioned at the beginning.

Although I only set out to help myself, on my journey I found the recipe for freedom from the fear and despair which ravage the world. These are our modern plagues, spread by incessant news of political upheaval, displacement of peoples, climate change, and resource insufficiency. Their affects are mental health issues on an unprecedented scale – countless people trapped in heart places of fear, hopelessness and the gloom that diminishes man.

But we were not created for crippling by these emotions or the thinking that feeds them. Their antidote is hope and joy in mind and heart. Knowing this as I now do, I would be selfish if I kept the truth to myself. That is that there are towering gates to hope and joy which can be freely opened by the people of God. They offer the world rescue from an inferior life into fullness of life. It is within reach, on the other side of the gates.

Their opening is not so much an option as an imperative. Why? Because too much is at stake if we don't. Lives will be lost in the darkness of addiction and suicide, or simply lived in misery. Not only does that carry a personal cost for those affected, but an ominous societal impact. Bear in mind that the younger generations currently struggling with mental health issues will be tomorrow's leaders. For all our sakes, for the sake of generations to come, they need to be well.

Against that backdrop, the stirring I hear within me goes like this, 'We must refuse the narrative of our time. We must begin a movement towards hope and joy which will transform the world.'

Imagine a group of people equipped in this way. How might that impact society, workplaces, cities, nations? Better health, increased productivity, less crime, reduced addiction and suicide rates… to name a few.

What if you and I began to dream the impossible with God, who does the immeasurably more than we could ask or imagine?

Are there levels of hope which will eradicate famine or depression? Or could a well of joy be struck which would quash wars? Crazy questions perhaps but could it be that the ones who dare ask them will find the necessary, out of the box, answers.

Pushing farther, dare we ask God to live His wildest, solution-laded dreams through us?

Make no mistake that the world, desperate for light, will flock towards hope and joy carriers like bees to a honey pot.

Could the biggest news become that a hope and joy movement has begun that has become unstoppable?

In the Bible, we repeatedly see one person with courage and conviction stepping forwards and changing everything. Daniel, Nehemiah, Joseph, Samson, innumerable others. How? First, they saw and dreamed about what might be. Second, they risked everything for it, and third, when they did heaven backed them.

I never imagined running into hope and joy would lead me to this thrilling place of experience and understanding. But now it has, I can only hear heaven's loud drum-beat calling for pioneers to catalyse this movement. And amidst the unknowns which might deter us, the known is that heaven will be with us if we do.

Perhaps like a soldier who feels compelled to defend his nation, I find myself compelled to volunteer to be one who will release bottomless hope and joy.

Will you?